English G 21

Klassenarbeitstrainer
für Schülerinnen und Schüler

**mit Lösungen
Lerntipps
Kompetenztest**

Deine **Audios** findest du hier:

1. Gehe auf scook.de.
2. Gib den unten stehenden Zugangscode in die Box ein.
3. Hab viel Spaß mit den Audios.

Dein Zugangscode auf
www.scook.de | 67oqx-4f4ko

English G 21 • Band D 2

Klassenarbeitstrainer mit Lösungen und Lerntipps

Konzeption
Dr. Ursula Mulla und Nogi Mulla, Germering

Erarbeitet von
Bärbel Schweitzer, M.A., Staufen

In Zusammenarbeit mit der Englischredaktion
Dr. Christiane Kallenbach (Projektleitung)
Stefanie Bayer
Susanne Bennetreu (Bildredaktion)

Beratende Mitwirkung
Angela Ringel-Eichinger, Bietigheim-Bissingen
Martina Schroeder, Stedtlingen
Bernd Sold, Bobenheim-Roxheim

Illustrationen
Constanze Schargan, Berlin
Roland Beier, Berlin (Lösungseinleger S. 29)

Bildquellen
Alamy, Abingdon (S. 8 boat: Michael Howard; S. 8 Oxford Street: PCL; Education Photos, Guildford (S. 21 fashion show: John Walmsley); Anthony Grimley, Bath (S. 37 fun run); Istock, Calgary (S. 50 bike: David Morgan); Photolibrary, New York (S. 8 Buckingham Palace: Charles Bowman; S. 33 boy: Hans Carlen); Rob Cousins, Bristol (S. 83 kids in canteen, S. 44 hamster); Shutterstock, New York (S. 8 beach: Augustinho Goncalves; S. 17 Big Ben: Jenny Horne; S. 33, 39 dog: Eric Isselee; S. 33, 39 cat: Myth Photography; S. 33 elderly lady: Yuri Acurs; S. 33 young lady: Factoria singular fotografia; S. 33 girl: Elene Elisseeva; S. 33 rabbit: Reddogs; S. 33 mouse: Ljupco Smokovski; S. 33 budgie: Eric Isselee; S. 39 guinea pig: Sascha Burkard; S. 42 cat on sofa: Pavel Sazonov; S. 46 boy: Yuri Acurs; S. 46 girl with dark hair: Konstantin Sutyagin; S. 46 girl with blond hair: Mityukhin Oleg Petrovich; S. 50 accident: Toa55; S. 50 black car: Ben Smith; S. 50 white car: Vibrant Image Studio; S. 62 man: Elene Elisseeva; S. 66 woman: Andresr; S. 66 teen girl: @erics; S. 66 man: Carsten Reisinger; S. 66 boy: Galina Barskaya)

Titelbild
Constanze Schargan, Berlin; IFA-Bilderteam, Ottobrunn (Hintergrund Union Jack: Jon Arnold Images)

Layout und technische Umsetzung
Heike Freund, Hameln

Umschlaggestaltung
Klein & Halm Grafikdesign, Berlin

www.cornelsen.de
www.EnglishG.de

1. Auflage, 9. Druck 2019

© 2008 Cornelsen Verlag, Berlin
© 2018 Cornelsen Verlag GmbH, Berlin

Das Werk und seine Teile sind urheberrechtlich geschützt.
Jede Nutzung in anderen als den gesetzlich zugelassenen Fällen bedarf der vorherigen schriftlichen Einwilligung des Verlages.
Hinweis zu §§ 60a, 60b UrhG: Weder das Werk noch seine Teile dürfen ohne eine solche Einwilligung an Schulen oder in Unterrichts- und Lehrmedien (§ 60b Abs. 3 UrhG) vervielfältigt, insbesondere kopiert oder eingescannt, verbreitet oder in ein Netzwerk eingestellt oder sonst öffentlich zugänglich gemacht oder wiedergegeben werden. Dies gilt auch für Intranets von Schulen.

Druck: H. Heenemann, Berlin

ISBN 978-3-06-031904-6

INHALT

Unit	Klassenarbeit	Seite
Welcome	**Klassenarbeit** Listening • Language • Writing • Speaking	5
Unit 1	**Klassenarbeit A** Reading • Language • Mediation	10
	Klassenarbeit B Listening • Language • Writing • Speaking	15
Unit 2	**Klassenarbeit A** Reading • Language • Mediation	21
	Klassenarbeit B Listening • Language • Writing • Speaking	27
Unit 3	**Klassenarbeit A** Listening • Language • Writing	33
	Klassenarbeit B Reading • Language • Mediation • Speaking	38
Unit 4	**Klassenarbeit A** Reading • Language • Mediation	45
	Klassenarbeit B Listening • Language • Writing • Speaking	50
Unit 5	**Klassenarbeit A** Listening • Language • Writing	56
	Klassenarbeit B Reading • Language • Mediation • Speaking	60
Unit 6	**Klassenarbeit A** Reading • Language • Mediation • Speaking	66
	Klassenarbeit B Listening • Language • Writing	72
Zusatz	**Kompetenztest** Listening • Speaking • Reading • Writing	78

ZUERST EIN PAAR BEMERKUNGEN ...

Liebe Schülerin, lieber Schüler,

in diesem Klassenarbeitstrainer findest du zu jeder Unit zwei Klassenarbeiten, mit denen du alle Fertigkeiten (skills) trainieren kannst, die du für die Klassenarbeiten benötigst.
Das Üben für eine Klassenarbeit ist wie ein Puzzle: du brauchst mehrere Teile, die – zu einem Ganzen zusammengesetzt – deine optimale Vorbereitung sind.

Vorbereitung
Plane genügend Zeit ein. Mache einen Lernplan vor der Klassenarbeit. Hole dir bei Unklarheiten Hilfe. Am Tag vor der Arbeit wiederholst du nur kurz.

Lernheft
Besorge dir ein Schreibheft. Es dient für Schreibaufgaben und zusätzliche Übungen. Schreibe schön und übersichtlich (mit Überschrift, Aufgabe, Seite). Lege ein Inhaltsverzeichnis auf der 1. Seite an.

Lösungsheft
Vergleiche deine Lösungen mit den Musterlösungen. Hier findest du auch die Hörtexte und Lerntipps mit weiteren Übungen.

Wiederholung
Aufgaben, die dir noch schwer fallen, solltest du ein zweites oder drittes Mal machen.

Punkteschlüssel
Er hilft dir, deine Leistung einzuschätzen.

Listening Aufgaben
Lies Überschrift und Aufgaben in Ruhe durch. Höre den Text an. Bearbeite dann die Aufgaben. Höre den Text noch einmal an. Bearbeite die noch fehlenden Aufgaben.

Reading Aufgaben
Lies Überschrift und Text in Ruhe durch. Lies die Aufgaben, ohne sie zu bearbeiten. Lies den Text noch einmal. Markiere passende Stellen mit verschiedenen Farben! Bearbeite jetzt die Aufgaben.

Writing Aufgaben / Mediation Aufgaben
Lies die Aufgabe genau durch. Beachte Hilfestellungen in der Aufgabe. Notiere dir Stichworte. Schreibe deinen Text. Überprüfe ihn auf Vollständigkeit, Rechtschreibung und richtige Grammatik.

Speaking Aufgaben
Lies die Aufgabenstellung. Höre den Text an.
Sprich beim 2. Hören mit.

Wenn du regelmäßig übst, gewinnst du an Sicherheit bei der Bearbeitung der unterschiedlichen Aufgaben. Und: je besser du wirst, umso mehr Freude hast du beim Lernen und natürlich auch mit der englischen Sprache.

Übrigens: die Klassenarbeiten in diesem Heft prüfen das Gelernte sehr ausführlich ab. Du brauchst daher für die Bearbeitung länger als eine Schulstunde. Natürlich kannst du dir die Klassenarbeiten auch auf einzelne Tage aufteilen oder bestimmte Aufgaben ganz gezielt üben.

So, am besten, du fängst gleich an.

Ich wünsche dir viel Freude mit dem Klassenarbeitstrainer und ein erfolgreiches, gutes Schuljahr.

Have fun with English!

Bärbel Schweitzer

# Klassenarbeit

Welcome back

5

Gesamtpunktzahl mit Speaking _____ / 65 Note _____

Gesamtpunktzahl ohne Speaking _____ / 55 Note _____

LISTENING

_____ / 25

 01 Paul's very special holiday

You are listening to a radio programme. A reporter is interviewing Paul, a 13-year-old boy from Southampton.

> Lies im Vorwort, wie du **Listening**-Aufgaben gut lösen kannst.
> Du kannst diese Aufgabe auch als **Reading**-Aufgabe machen.
> Lies dazu den Hörtext im **Lösungsheft** auf S. 2 und bearbeite dann die Aufgabe.

1 Where did Paul go?

_____ / 7

Look at the map (Landkarte) first. Then listen carefully. Put a cross (✗) in the countries where Paul went.

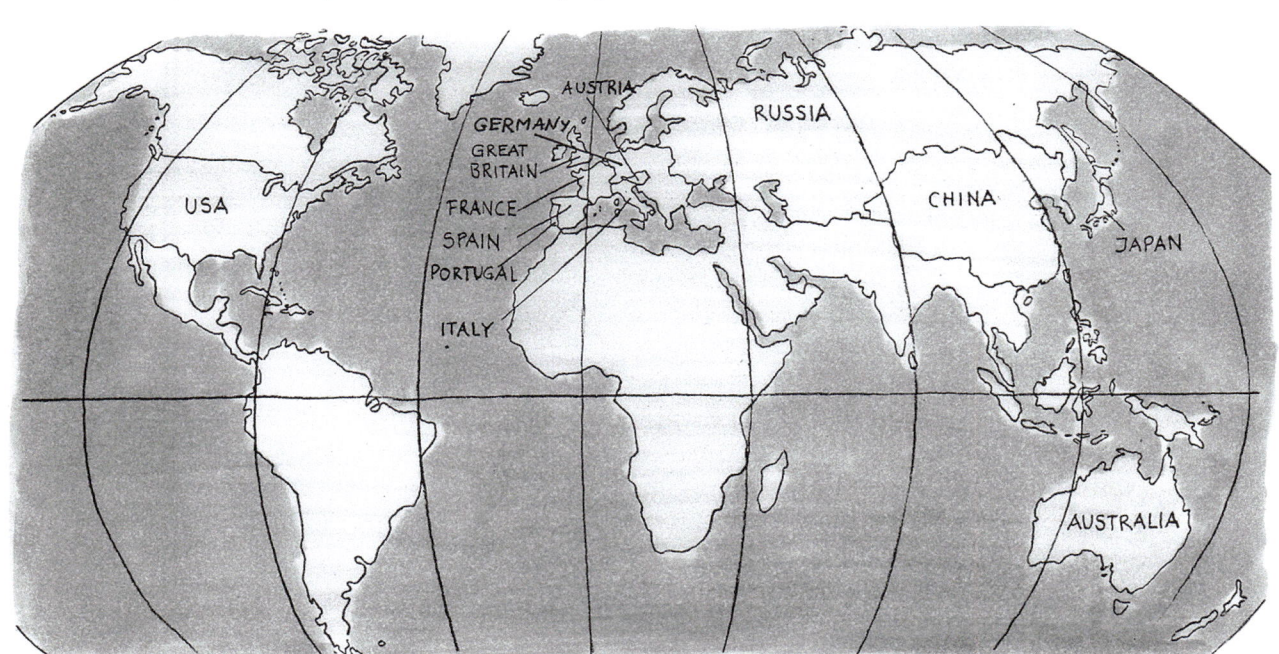

2 What was the weather like?

___ / 8

Listen again, then tick (✔) the correct answer. Sometimes you must tick two boxes.

	warm	cold	sunny	rainy	hot	windy	stormy
Paris	☐	☐	☐	☐	☐	☐	☐
Berlin	☐	☐	☐	☐	☐	☐	☐
Munich *(München)*	☐	☐	☐	☐	☐	☐	☐
Rome *(Rom)*	☐	☐	☐	☐	☐	☐	☐
New York	☐	☐	☐	☐	☐	☐	☐
Miami	☐	☐	☐	☐	☐	☐	☐
Beijing *(Peking)*	☐	☐	☐	☐	☐	☐	☐
Sydney	☐	☐	☐	☐	☐	☐	☐

3 What do you know about Paul's holiday?

___ / 10

Read the sentences first. Then listen again and tick (✔) the correct box.

		Right	Wrong
1	Paul went on holidays with his parents.	☐	☐
2	Paul liked the museums in Berlin.	☐	☐
3	Paul can speak French.	☐	☐
4	Paul went to a museum in Munich.	☐	☐
5	Paul wants to go to Munich again.	☐	☐
6	The Italians were nice.	☐	☐
7	Paul didn't like Miami.	☐	☐
8	Paul was in China for one week.	☐	☐
9	Paul's uncle lives in Shanghai.	☐	☐
10	In Sydney it was wintertime and very cold.	☐	☐

Welcome back | Klassenarbeit

LANGUAGE

___ / 20

1 WORDS Holiday words

___ / 12

Find the words.

Spain is a __ __ __ __ __ __ .

There are three __ __ __ __ __ __ in the __ __ __ .

From up there you have a good __ __ __ __ .

Is the __ __ __ __ __ empty?

Yes, there is __ __ __ __ __ __ there.

Look, there is a little __ __ __ __ __ __

in the lake.

You live in a country and you go to another

country – you go __ __ __ __ __ __ __ __ .

Every August we stay in our

__ __ __ __ __ __ __ by the __ __ .

Mr and Mrs Miller always __ __ __ __ to Portugal.

Can you make a word with the letters in the boxes ?
Put them in the right order.

 **t**

2 WORDS Irregular simple past forms

___/8

Fill in the infinitive, the irregular simple past form or the German translation.

Infinitive	Simple past form	German translation
		sich treffen
	shone	
		schwimmen
put		
	read	
		essen
ride		
throw		

WRITING

___/10

A holiday postcard

You want to write a postcard to your friend Paul Wells in Edinburgh.
Choose one of the postcards and tell him:

– where you are
– where you are staying
– what you did yesterday
– what you want to do today
– what the weather is like
– how long you are there

Write **6 or more** sentences and an ending into the postcard on p. 9.

Welcome back | Klassenarbeit

Dear Paul,

_____

_____

_____

_____

_____

_____

_____

_____

Paul Wells

3, Arnhem Drive

Edinburgh EH2 2DG

SPEAKING ____/10

🎧 02 Talking about the holidays

It's the first day at school after the holidays. The new teacher Mr Hall is talking to the class. At the moment he is talking to Jenny. He is asking her questions about her holidays.

First listen to Mr Hall and Jenny.

🎧 03 Now you

Now Mr Hall is interviewing you.
Listen to his questions, then answer in complete sentences.
Drücke die Pausentaste, damit du Zeit für deine Antwort hast.

Use these notes for your answers:

- Ihr seid nach Italien gefahren. (1)
- Ihr seid mit dem Auto gefahren. (1)
- In der ersten Woche war das Wetter sehr warm und sonnig, an einem Tag sogar über dreißig Grad. In der zweiten Woche war es bewölkt, an einem Tag regnete es. (2x 1,5)
- Ihr habt in eurem Wohnwagen gewohnt. (1,5)
- Als das Wetter schlecht war, seid ihr in ein Museum gegangen. Sage auch, in welches Museum ihr gegangen seid, z. B. ins Spaghettimuseum. (2,5)
- Ihr wart zwei Wochen weg. (1)

Unit 1 — Klassenarbeit A

Gesamtpunktzahl _____ / 65   Note _____

READING

_____ / 10

Bristol Times   September 20

Back to school

School started again last week. We asked our readers to tell us about their holidays. Here is one of the letters:

Well, holidays are sometimes difficult for the families: parents have to go to work but there is no school for the children. The problem is that many children watch television all day. So this year our children Ben (7) and David (12) went to Bristol Summer Camp. They were there from 10 o'clock in the morning to 5 o'clock in the afternoon from Monday to Friday.

They did lots of interesting things. Both Ben and David loved going to the summer camp from the first day. I can't think of a day when they didn't want to go.

Let me give you two examples of what they did. One day they worked on a "pirate ship", the next day they played on it and they read stories about pirates.
It was super for the kids!!!

Another day was "Radio Day". First they went to *Radio Bristol*, where they found out everything about the radio, and the next day they worked on their own radio programme. You could listen to it last Friday. It was great.

I can only say: the kids liked the summer camp and we, the parents, liked it, too!!!

Mrs Sue Lewis, Bristol

1 What did they do in the summer camp?   _____ / 4

Tick (✔) the two summer camp activities that Mrs Lewis wrote about.

1

2

3

4

2 Right – wrong?

___ / 6

Tick (✔) the correct box.

		Right	Wrong
1	The holidays are over.	☐	☐
2	In the holidays Ben and David watched TV all day.	☐	☐
3	They were at the camp for 5 hours from Monday to Friday.	☐	☐
4	The children didn't want to go to the camp at first.	☐	☐
5	They went to a café called "The Pirate Ship".	☐	☐
6	The summer camp's radio programme was good.	☐	☐

LANGUAGE

___ / 43

1 STUDY SKILLS Describing pictures

___ / 14

Look at the picture and describe it. Use the words below for describing pictures and follow the numbers to complete the sentences.

1 At the bottom of the picture there is the _____.

2 _____ there is a café.

3 _____ a family is sitting _____ the café.

4 _____ a young man _____.

5 _____ there are two girls. A young boy with a _____ is walking _____ them.

6 _____ there is an old _____.

7 _____ I can see a _____ in the _____.

> **Useful words:**
> on the left • on the right • at the top • at the bottom • in the middle • in the background • in the foreground • there is • there are
>
> **Tipp:**
> Um zu sagen, was gerade passiert, benutze das **present progressive**: Jo **is talking** to Jack.

2 WORDS Irregular verbs ____ / 8

Fill in the missing forms of the irregular verbs.

Infinitive	Simple past form	German translation
	rode	
		holen, besorgen
teach		
		hören
	gave	
see		
	spoke	
		fliegen

3 GRAMMAR After the first week at the summer camp ____ / 13

*The first week at the summer camp is over. Ben and David tell their friends about the first week.
Complete what Ben and David said.
Use the **simple past**. Be careful: sometimes you must use a negative form.*

On Monday morning we _____ (get up) at 7.30 and _____ (go) to the

camp for the first time. There _____ (be) 40 boys and girls at the camp. Most of them

_____ (come) from Bristol but some of them _____ (not/be) from our

school. In the afternoon we _____ (work) on the pirate ship. That _____

(be) great. On Tuesday we _____ (not/work) on the ship. On Wednesday and Thursday we

_____ (read) stories about pirates. After that we _____ (play) on our ship

and _____ (have) a really good time. We _____ (not/read) comics and we

_____ (not/stay) in bed all day long.

 Bei dieser Übung und der nächsten geht es um das **simple past**. Du sollst **bejahte Aussagesätze** (positive statements) und **verneinte Aussagesätze** (negative statements) bilden. Lies dazu noch einmal die **Grammar Files** 1 und 2 in deinem Englischbuch auf S. 133/134.

Unit 1 | Klassenarbeit A   13

4 GRAMMAR What Ben and David did and what they didn't do   ____ / 8

Here are some pictures of what the two brothers did at the summer camp and what they didn't do.
*Write positive and negative statements in the **simple past**. Use the words from the box. You don't need all of them.*

| play computer • teach • go by train • work on • watch • go surfing • |
| speak • read • go by bus • get up • go by bike • meet new friends |

1 _____   2 _____

3 _____   4 _____

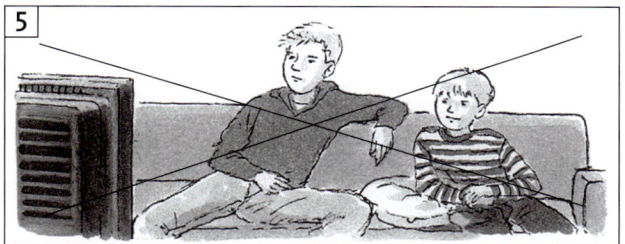 

5 _____   6 _____

7 _____   8 _____

☞ **Simple past positive statements**
Regelmäßige Verben: stay ► stay**ed**
Unregelmäßige Verben: meet ► **met** (2. Form)

Simple past negative statements
didn't + Infinitiv: he **didn't stay,** she **didn't meet**

Unit 1 | Klassenarbeit A

MEDIATION

____/12

David helps his brother Ben

At Bristol Summer Camp there are lots of boys and girls. Ben likes playing with Florian, a seven-year-old boy from Germany. Florian doesn't speak much English and Ben doesn't speak any German. So David helps them. Complete the dialogue.

Ben It's nice that you are here in our summer camp, Florian. Are you on holiday here in Bristol?

David Ben sagt, dass es schön ist, dass du _____

_____

Florian Ja, ich bin für zwei Wochen hier. Ich wohne im Haus meiner Tante hier in Bristol.

David He says that he is here _____. He is _____

_____

Ben And where does his/your aunt live?

David Und wo _____

Florian Sie wohnt hinter der Kirche in der Cumberland Street Nummer 7.

David She _____

Ben Well, that's great. We only live a mile away. We can come here together in the mornings. We always go by bike.

David _____

_____

Florian Ja, das ist eine gute Idee. Wir können auch heute gleich nach dem Summer Camp zusammen nach Hause gehen.

David He likes the idea. He says we can _____.

_____

Ben Yes, we can. But now we must help with the lunch. Let's go.

Klassenarbeit B

Unit 1

15

Gesamtpunktzahl ohne Speaking _____ / 70 Note _____

Gesamtpunktzahl mit Speaking _____ / 85 Note _____

LISTENING

_____ / 13

🎧 04 **Bristol today**

☞ Du kannst diese Aufgabe auch als **Reading**-Aufgabe machen. Du findest den Text auf S. 9 im Lösungsheft abgedruckt.

1 At the summer camps

_____ / 5

Listen to the radio programme "Bristol Today". Find out how long the children stayed at which summer camp. Tick (✔) the correct box.

	How long?			Which summer camp?				
	1 week	2 weeks	3 weeks	football camp	Bristol Summer Camp	riding camp	circus[1] camp	music camp
Sarah	☐	☐	☐	☐	☐	☐	☐	☐
Peter	☐	☐	☐	☐	☐	☐	☐	☐
Jason	☐	☐	☐	☐	☐	☐	☐	☐
Simon	☐	☐	☐	☐	☐	☐	☐	☐
David	☐	☐	☐	☐	☐	☐	☐	☐

[1] circus ['sɜːkəs]   Zirkus

2 The children and their holidays ___/8

*Listen again and find the **eight correct** statements. Please tick (✔) them.*

Sarah	a) was at a camp in Scotland for two weeks.	☐
	b) went horse riding in the afternoons.	☐
	c) cleaned the horses in the mornings and in the afternoons.	☐
	d) thinks that one week is not long enough.	☐
Peter	a) went to a circus one day.	☐
	b) learned everything about dogs.	☐
	c) showed his parents what he learned at the camp.	☐
	d) says that his families and friends didn't like the camp.	☐
Jason	a) played football with boys and girls all day long.	☐
	b) practised hard and learned many things.	☐
	c) says that three weeks is too long.	☐
	d) wants to go to a football camp again.	☐
Simon	a) says that his camp was in a school.	☐
	b) didn't like the rooms.	☐
	c) says that there were boys and girls from all parts of Britain at his camp.	☐
	d) and the other boys and girls played in a musical.	☐
David	a) stayed at the camp day and night.	☐
	b) only went to the camp in the afternoons.	☐
	c) did lots of interesting activities.	☐
	d) rode his bike.	☐

LANGUAGE ___/37

1 GRAMMAR Lunch break at school ___/5

The boys and girls of Cotham School are talking about their holidays.
*Complete the dialogue with **was/wasn't/were/weren't**.*

David My brother and I _____ at Bristol

Summer Camp. It _____ great.

What about you, where _____ you?

Susan My parents and I _____ in Spain.

It _____ hot and sunny. We _____ there for long, only for 10 days.

Jeremy So, the weather _____ good in Spain. I _____ in Ireland.

It _____ hot and sunny there, it _____ very wet and windy.

> **Simple past von (to) be**
> Beim **simple past** von **(to) be** gibt es nur zwei Formen:
> I, he, she, it was
> you, we, they were

2 GRAMMAR About the weekend

___/6

*It's Monday and Sally is asking Charlie about his weekend.
Complete Sally's questions with the correct question word.*

> **Question words**
> where, what, who, when, why

1 **Sally**   _____ did you go at the weekend, Charlie?

   Charlie I was in London.

2 **Sally**   _____ did you go with?

   Charlie I went with my aunt and uncle from Oxford.

3 **Sally**   _____ did you stay in London?

   Charlie We stayed at a big hotel outside London.

4 **Sally**   _____ did you stay outside London?

   Charlie Because it was not so expensive.

5 **Sally**   _____ did you come back home from London?

   Charlie At 8 o'clock on Sunday evening.

6 **Sally**   And ..., _____ do you think about London?

   Charlie Well, what a question, it was just great, great, great!!!

3 GRAMMAR An interview

____/ 14

George is at Southend Comprehensive School. Today he wants to interview his form teacher Mr Wilson for the school magazine. Write down his questions for the interview on the note pad.

George wants to ask his form teacher

1. about his **past**
   - when – come to this school
   - why – want to be a teacher
   - – go to school in Bristol
   - where – stay in your last holidays

2. about his life as a teacher **today**
   - what – teach
   - – like your job
   - when – get up in the morning
   - what – do in your free time

Notes for the interview

Past:

When did you come to this school?

_____

_____

_____

Today:

_____

_____

_____

_____

> ☞ Beachte bei dieser Übung, dass du sowohl Fragen im **simple present** (today) als auch im **simple past** (past) bilden sollst.
>
> **Fragen** mit **do/does** – **simple present**
> 1 ohne Fragewort ▶ **Do** you sing?
> 2 mit Fragewort ▶ **What do** you sing?
>
> **Fragen** mit **did** – **simple past**
> 1 ohne Fragewort ▶ **Did** you sing?
> 2 mit Fragewort ▶ **What did** you sing?

4 WORDS Irregular verbs

____/ 8

Find eight irregular verbs and write the infinitive, the simple past form and the German translation of the infinitive.

Infinitive	Simple past form	German translation
1 h *ear*	_____	_____
2 t_____	_____	_____
3 d_____	_____	_____
4 k_____	_____	_____
5 m_____	_____	_____
6 r_____	_____	_____
7 s_____	_____	_____
8 e_____	_____	_____

5 WORDS Say it in English

___/4

Was sagst du, wenn du ...

1 zu jemandem sagen willst, er oder sie solle sich um seine/ihre eigenen Angelegenheiten kümmern?

_____.

2 zu jemandem sagen willst, dass etwas überhaupt nicht in Frage kommt?

_____.

3 zu jemandem sagen willst: „Na, hör mal!"?

_____.

4 jemanden fragen willst, ob er/sie das wirklich glaubt?

_____.

WRITING

___/20

An e-mail to Germany

Simon is an English boy from Bristol. In his holidays he was in Scotland at an international music camp. He met Kai, a boy from Munich, Germany. At the end of September he writes an e-mail to Kai.

Er schreibt,

- wann er wieder mit der Schule begann und was es Neues aus der Schule gibt,
- dass er das *international music camp* super fand,
- dass er viel gelernt hat,
- dass er gerne mal wieder in ein *music camp* gehen möchte.

Er fragt Kai,

- ob es Kai im *music camp* auch gefallen hat,
- ob er wieder mal nach Großbritannien kommen möchte,
- ob er auch viel Englisch in Schottland gelernt hat,
- was er in den letzten zwei Wochen seiner Ferien gemacht hat.

Er bittet Kai,

- ihm etwas aus der deutschen Schule zu erzählen.

*Beginne und beende deine E-Mail.
Schreibe den Text der E-Mail in dein Lernheft.*

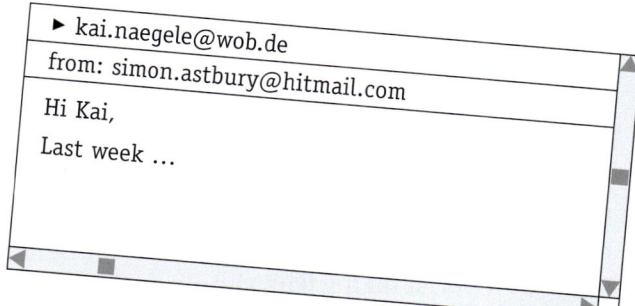

Unit 1 | Klassenarbeit B

SPEAKING

____/15

🎧 05 **Last Sunday**

Sarah, Susan, Tim and David are talking about last Sunday. Listen to Sarah.

Now you

Now you take David's part. Look at the ideas in the box. Choose some of them or think of new ideas. Take notes about David's Sunday from morning to night in the calendar. Write down **ten notes**.

> **Ideas:**
> help my mother/father/brother • play basketball • read books • meet my friends • do my homework • watch TV • have breakfast with … • have lunch • have tea • go to my friend/grandma • go to a museum … • play football • talk on the phone to … • tidy my room

4 October — *Sunday*

8.00	got up …
9.00	had breakfast with …
10.00	
11.00	
12.00	
13.00	
14.00	
15.00	
16.00	
17.00	
18.00	
19.00	
20.00	
21.00	

☞ ☐ Höre dir Sarahs Ausführungen nochmal genau an. Schreibe dir alle **Zeitangaben** (time phrases) und alle **Bindewörter** (linking words) heraus. Du findest den Text auch auf S. 12 im Lösungsteil.
☐ Baue sie in deine Ausführungen ein. Benutze unterschiedliche Satzanfänge, z.B. in the morning, after breakfast, at 11 o'clock, then, before, …
☐ Wie Sarah musst du auch im **simple past** sprechen.

Now tell Sarah, Susan and Tim about last Sunday. You are David. Say about ten sentences.

Klassenarbeit A — Unit 2

READING

Gesamtpunktzahl _____ / 70   Note _____

_____ / 22

Last month Becca Green wrote an article for the school magazine.

This year's fashion show – a hit
by Becca Green, Form 9 TG

Our school always has a fashion show in October. This year it was really fantastic. Forms 8, 9 and 10 invited the other students, the teachers and all the parents and grandparents. The assembly hall[1] was more than full – there were about 600 people. Everybody wanted to see this year's ideas. The 'models' were nervous, but our presenter Luke Smith from Form 10AR was even more nervous.

He was the most nervous person of all! But after the first two minutes he relaxed and was the best presenter ever. He explained[2] the different parts of the show and was funny at the same time.

The forms thought of the most interesting topics for the fashion show. Form 8 HG showed wonderful clothes from India, and did an Indian dance. The girls looked so beautiful. Form 9 TG made hats from different materials: newspapers, paper bags, old CDs. You could see big and small hats, funny and elegant hats. Their 'school hats' were really a highlight. They designed ten special hats for our school uniform. It was only a joke but everybody liked the idea. Form 10 FR's topic was 'new attics' and they showed fashions from the 1980s. Presenter Luke explained that most of these clothes were over 20 years old and came from their parents' attics. The grandparents had fun when they saw their children's old dresses, trousers, T-shirts and blouses again!

Another good thing was that the forms had great music for the show. Form 8 HG had slow and quiet Indian music, 9 TG sang songs about hats in their presentation and 10 FR had CDs from the 1980s. The parents and grandparents sang to the music, and even some of the teachers sang too!

Well, this year's fashion show was a hit. Thank you to all the boys and girls of the organisation team.

---

[1] assembly hall [əˈsemblɪ hɔːl] *Aula*   [2] (to) explain sth. [ɪksˈpleɪn] *etwas erklären*

Unit 2 | Klassenarbeit A

1 The fashion show ___/12

Fill in the mind map with information from the text.

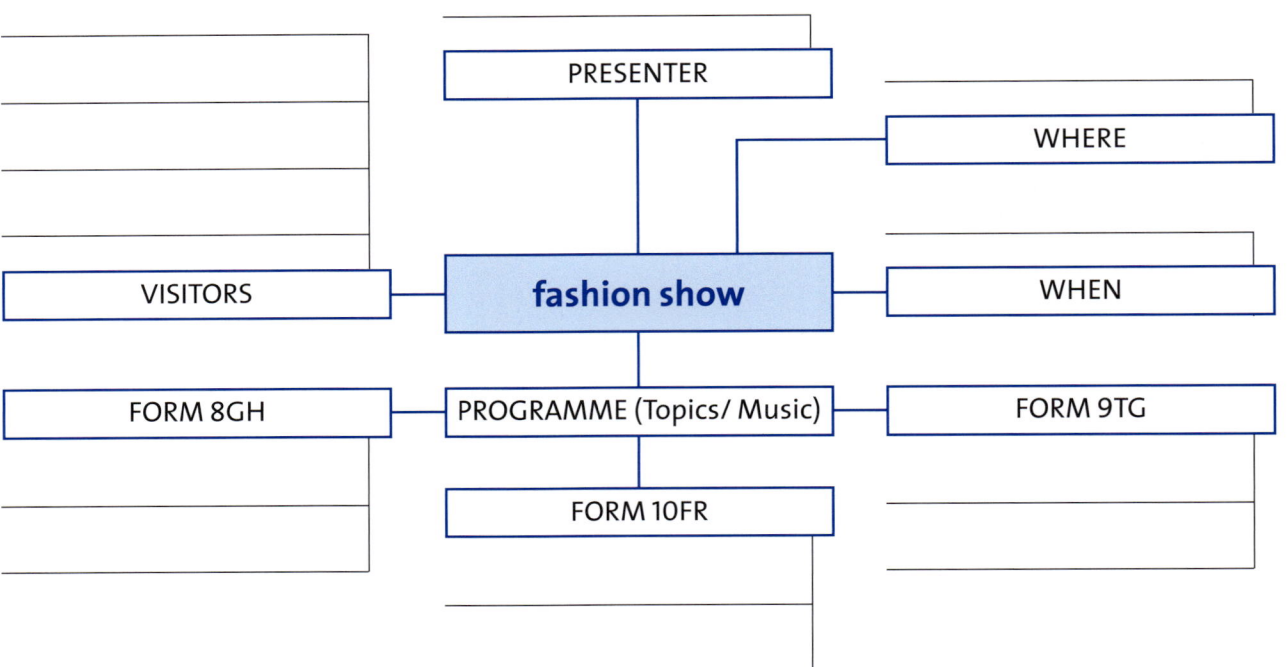

2 More about the fashion show ___/10

Put 17 ticks (✔) in the correct boxes.

☞ In jeder Zeile findest du die Angabe in Klammern, wie viele Häkchen du machen musst.

The school	The models	Luke Smith	The show	Form 8 HG	Form 9 TG	Form 10 FR	The parents	The grandparents	The teachers	
										had music from a CD. (2)
										was one of the best shows in the last years. (1)
										explained why the name for the fashion of Form 10 FR was 'new attics'. (1)
										sang while the models presented. (4)
										presented old-fashioned clothes. (1)
										has a fashion show every year. (1)
										was/were very nervous. (2)
										had a topic for their show. (3)
										presented fashion from another country. (1)
										showed hats from recycled material. (1)

Unit 2 | Klassenarbeit A   23

LANGUAGE

___ / 37

1 WORDS What people said after the fashion show

___ / 7

Fill in the correct words. Be careful – there are two words in the box that you don't need.

> fed up with • love • recycling • presenter • even •
> more than • join • everybody • cheap

Betty I _____ fashion shows – they're fantastic. Luke was our _____.

He was great.

Susan There were _____ 600 people in the assembly hall!

_____ liked the fashion show!

Mr Hall Why didn't you _____ me, Susan? The show was super.

John I thought, oh no, not another boring fashion show. I was _____ fashion shows.

But this one was different.

Form teacher Great idea, form 9TG – you used old stuff for new hats. A great example of _____.

2 WORDS Clothes

___ / 12

Fill in the chart with words that have to do with clothes. Find **four** words or more each.

Clothes		
What you can wear: (nouns)	What you can do with them: (verbs)	How you can describe them: (adjectives)
1 hat	1 buy	1 warm
2	2	2
3	3	3
4	4	4
5	5	5

3 GRAMMAR This year's fashion show   ___/7

Here is what Joe said about the fashion show. Complete the sentences with the right forms of the adjectives.

The fashion show was super!! The colours of the Indian clothes were _____ (beautiful) than the others. The music of form 8 HG was _____ (quiet) than the music of the other forms. The hats of 9 TG were _____ (cheap) than the clothes of 8 HG and 10 FR. I think our school uniform can look _____ (funny) with one of the hats. But with a hat it is _____ (expensive) than at the moment. There were _____ (many) topics than the years before. This year's fashion show was _____ (good) than last year's show.

4 GRAMMAR What do you think?   ___/3

Write complete sentences and choose adjectives from the box.

| nice • interesting • boring • difficult • exciting |

Example: football match – fashion show

I think a football match is more interesting than a fashion show.

1 skirt – trousers

_____

2 English – Maths

_____

3 computer games – TV

_____

☞ **a) Comparison with -er/est:** Einsilbige Adjektive/Adjektive auf -y
   young – younger – youngest
   late – later – latest
   hot – hotter – hottest
   pretty – prettier – prettiest

b) Comparison with more/most: Andere zwei- und mehrsilbige Adjektive
   boring – more boring – most boring
   difficult – more difficult – most difficult

c) Irregular comparison:
   good – better – best
   bad – worse – worst
   much/many – more – most

5 GRAMMAR Before the fashion show

___/8

*Lucy and Claire from 9 TG are talking about the fashion show.
Complete the sentences with the following possessive pronouns:*

> yours • mine • theirs • ours • hers

Lucy   Our show is a big surprise. What about the students of form 10 FR?

Do you know anything about _____?

Claire   No, I don't. But I know that _____ is great. Our hats are a super idea.

My mum helped me with my hat, so _____ is ready.

What about _____, Lucy? Is your hat ready?

Lucy   Well, _____ is almost ready. Did you see Jenny's hat? _____ is super.

Can I see _____ now, Claire?

Claire   So what do you think of my hat, Lucy?

Lucy   Wow, _____ is the best, really!

   Um das richtige Possessivpronomen herauszufinden, solltest du dir zunächst überlegen, welches Nomen ersetzt werden soll.
   Wähle dann das passende Pronomen aus.

   Beispiel:
   My birthday party was super. What about you? How was (**your birthday party** ▶) **yours**?

MEDIATION

___/10

Preparing the show

The students of Cotham School are preparing the fashion show.
Jessica, a German girl, is an exchange student[1] at Cotham school at the moment.
Her English is not so good. She wants some information about the show and talks to Lucy in form 9 TG.
You are an English student at Cotham School and help Jessica.

Jessica Was geschieht hier?

You Jessica wants to know what is happening here.

Lucy We're preparing our fashion show.

You Lucy sagt, _____.

Jessica Frag sie bitte, wer die Modenschau präsentiert.

You Jessica wants to know who _____.

Lucy Every year the boys and girls of the forms 8, 9 and 10 present it.

You Sie sagt, _____.

Jessica Ist eine Modenschau jedes Jahr nicht langweilig?

You She wants to know if (ob) a fashion year _____.

Lucy Sometimes yes. But this year every form has a different topic, so it can't be boring.

You _____.

Jessica Und wann ist die Modenschau? Ich möchte gerne kommen.

You _____.

Lucy Great. It's on Saturday evening.

You _____.

---

[1] exchange student [ɪksˈtʃeɪndʒ ˌstjuːdnt]   *Austauschschüler/in*

Klassenarbeit B

Unit 2

27

Gesamtpunktzahl ohne Speaking _____ / 65 Note _____

Gesamtpunktzahl mit Speaking _____ / 75 Note _____

LISTENING

_____ / 14

🎧 06 **Presentation of a project**

The students of form 7 DH are presenting their project 'Our school garden'. Listen to Mike, Sally and Carol.

> **New words**
> head teacher [ˌhed ˈtiːtʃə] *Schulleiter/in;* flower [ˈflaʊə] *Blume;* bench [bentʃ] *(Sitz-)Bank;* expert [ˈekspɜ] *Experte/Expertin;* plant [plɑːnt] *Pflanze*

1 The project

_____ / 8

What did they do in their project? Look at the pictures and put them in the right order:

Unit 2 | Klassenarbeit B

2 HEADS AND TAILS About the school garden   ___/6

*Listen again and match the heads and tails of these sentences. Draw lines.
There are two more endings than you need.*

1 Form 7 DH
2 The students and Mrs Wallace
3 When the head teacher agreed
4 The form needed help
5 The other students of the school
6 With the money from the cakes
7 At the end of the presentation

a) they worked together with other classes.
b) bought cakes in the school breaks.
c) everybody looked at the new school garden.
d) presented their project to their parents.
e) talked about the project together.
f) so they asked somebody from the flower shop.
g) they bought plants and flowers.
h) had lots of problems together.
i) they started with the school garden.

(Form 7 DH → d presented their project to their parents.)

LANGUAGE   ___/36

1 GRAMMAR Questions about the project   ___/6

*The guests in the new school garden ask a lot of questions about the project.
Complete their questions with **How much / How many**.*

1 _____ time did you have for the project?

2 _____ parents helped you with the project?

3 _____ money did you need for the plants?

4 _____ cakes did you make?

5 _____ sugar[1] did you need for all the cakes?

6 _____ students worked in the presentation group?

2 WORDS Say it in English   ___/6

1 Was ist los? _____

2 Du hast Unrecht. _____

3 Ich stimme dir zu. _____

4 Halt den Mund! _____

5 Was machst du gerade? _____

6 Mach kein Durcheinander. _____

---

[1] sugar [ˈsʊgə]   Zucker

3 WORDS Opposites ____/12

1 cheap ◄► _____   7 fast ◄► _____
2 better ◄► _____   8 (to) save money ◄► _____
3 right ◄► _____   9 (to) find ◄► _____
4 fantastic ◄► _____ 10 smaller ◄► _____
5 (to) finish ◄► _____ 11 clever ◄► _____
6 boring ◄► _____   12 (to) love ◄► _____

4 GRAMMAR What they can buy ____/8

The students of 7 DH talk about their garden project and what they want to buy for their garden. Look at the pictures and make comparisons. Write two sentences for each picture.

Example:

The apple cake is sweeter than the chocolate cake. The cheese cake is the sweetest.

good

beautiful

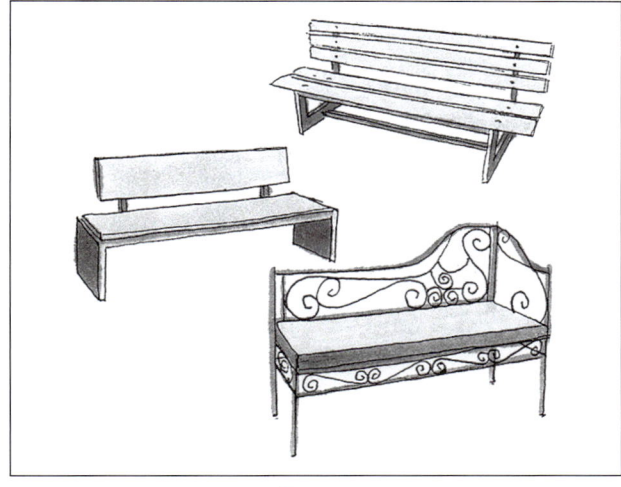

funny

The second bench is ...

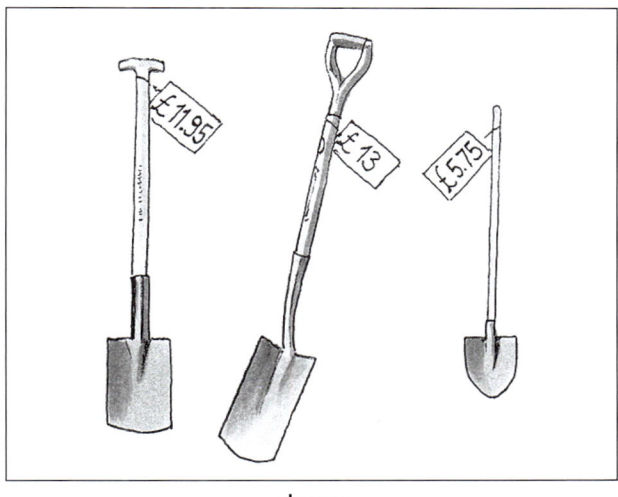

cheap

The first spade ...

Unit 2 | Klassenarbeit B

5 GRAMMAR About yourself

_____ / 4

Tell us about yourself and compare yourself to some people who you know.
*Use **4 different adjectives** and **4 different structures** (siehe Hinweishand).*

1 I'm *older than* my friend.

2 In my class I'm the _____ student.

3 I'm _____ my aunt/uncle.

4 I'm _____ my teacher.

5 I'm _____ my cousin/brother/sister.

  Comparison
- Sue is **as** old **as** Tim.
- Tom is older **than** Jeremy.
- Jeremy is **not as** old **as** Tom.
- Tom is **the** oldest.

WRITING

_____ / 15

An article for the school magazine

You are writing an article for the school magazine about the school garden project.
*Use the following key words and write at least **eight** complete sentences.*

1 topic – school garden
2 old garden – not nice
3 but! – no money
4 make and sell cakes – school – Bristol Market
5 need help – Mr Hull from the flower shop – parents
6 end of the project – presentation – parents
7 cakes and drink – say thank you

You can start like this:

The school garden
I'm writing about our school project. Our topic was ...

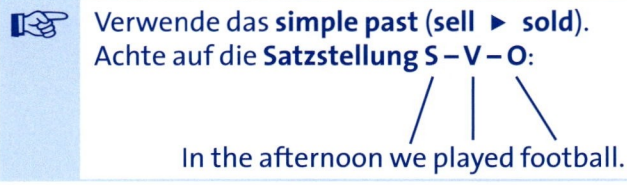
Verwende das **simple past** (sell ▶ sold).
Achte auf die **Satzstellung S – V – O**:
In the afternoon we played football.

Unit 2 | Klassenarbeit B | 31

SPEAKING

____ / 10

 07 **Two countries – two projects**

Sally is one of the students of 7 DH who did the school garden project. She tells you about the project and asks you questions about a project at your school. Listen to her and answer her questions.

> Höre dir Sallys Ausführungen und Fragen zuerst einmal an.
> Überlege dir anhand der Zeichnungen, wie du ihre Fragen beantworten kannst.
> Mache Notizen in die Tabelle auf S. 32.
> Höre dir dann den Text ein 2. Mal an und beantworte Sallys Fragen.
> Drücke dabei die Pausentaste, damit du Zeit für deine Antworten hast.

1 awful classroom – old lamps

2 paint classroom – put up new lamps

3 who could help? – get money from

4 flea market[1] – old books

5 one Saturday – parents and students – paint – put up new lamps – classroom

6 presentation – parents and teachers

[1] flea market ['fliː ˌmɑːkɪt] *Flohmarkt*

Sally's questions	Your ideas
What was your project about?	
Tell me why you started the project.	
What about your form, did you have any problems too?	
How did you get the money for the project?	
How did you go on with your project and who helped you?	
What about your presentation?	

Two countries – two projects

Sally Hi! I'm Sally, I'm from Bristol. I want to tell you something about our school garden project. What about you? What was your project about?

You Our project was …

Sally That's interesting. Let me tell you why we started our project. You see, we had this old school garden at our school. It looked awful. So one day we had the idea to make it nicer. But now tell me why you started your project.

You …

Sally Good idea. Now, we really had a problem because we needed an expert and we needed money for the plants. What about your form, did you have any problems, too?

You …

Sally We sold cakes at school and at the market in Bristol. How did you get the money for the project?

You …

Sally Good! When we had the money, we started working in the garden. It looks super now, really. How did you go on with your project and who helped you?

You …

Sally At the end we presented the project to our parents and the teachers. What about your presentation?

You …

Klassenarbeit A

Unit 3

33

Gesamtpunktzahl _____ / 55   Note _____

LISTENING

_____ / 16

 08 Pets in Bristol

Listen to a radio programme. Today people can call and talk about their pets.

> ☞ Lies in deinem Englischbuch das **Skills File** zu **Listening** auf S. 125 durch.
> Wenn du einen Signalton hörst, kannst du die Pausentaste drücken,
> um die Fragen in Aufgabe 1 und 2 zu beantworten.

1 Pets and people

_____ / 8

*Look at the photos and draw lines from the persons to the pet that they are talking about.
Then draw lines to the pets' names. Be careful: there are two more pets and four more pets' names than you need.*

Mrs Hall

(2x)

Pizza

??

Mary

Mr Benson

Mousy

Mrs Gray

Mickey

Noodle

Josh

Mr Bean

Polly

Unit 3 | Klassenarbeit A

2 About the radio programme   ___/8

Listen again. Tick (✔) the **eight correct** answers. There can be more than one correct answer.

☞ Lies in deinem Englischbuch das **Skills File** zu **Multiple-choice exercises** auf S. 124 durch.

In today's radio programme	a) the presenter asks questions about the callers' pets.	☐
	b) people can talk to the presenter.	☐
	c) only people with problems can call.	☐
Mrs Hall	a) liked going for a walk with her pet.	☐
	b) will be OK again next week.	☐
	c) has got a problem with her neighbour.	☐
Mary	a) always cleans the pet's cage.	☐
	b) sometimes helps her mum.	☐
	c) still goes to school.	☐
Mrs Gray	a) has got a problem with her pet.	☐
	b) and her neighbours have got a pet together.	☐
	c) is at home all day.	☐
Josh	a) has got a pet.	☐
	b) can't have a pet.	☐
	c) will get Mrs Hall's telephone number.	☐

LANGUAGE   ___/28

1 WORDS When you go on holiday   ___/9

Find the words and fill them in.

1 When you want to go on holiday you pack your clothes in a __ __ __ ☐ __ __ ☐ __ .

2 When you want to go by train and come back too you need a __ __ __ __ ☐ __ ☐ __ __ __ __ __ __ .

3 When you want to go on holiday and you have got a pet it's __ __ __ __ __ __ ☐ __ __

    that somebody looks after your pet.

4 The opposite of happy is __ __ __ .

5 The opposite of friend is ☐ __ __ __ __ __ .

6 If you are __ __ __ you can't go to school.

7 This bird lives in a tree: ☐ __ __ __ __ __ __ __ ☐ __ .

8 If you __ __ __ __ __ __ __ ☐ to do something you will do it and you must do it.

9 If you like somebody very much you can call him or her your ☐ ☐ ☐ ☐ ☐ h ☐ ☐ ☐ ☐ .

(You can make the word with the letters from the boxes if you put them in the right order.)

Unit 3 | Klassenarbeit A

2 WORDS Who is at the animal party?   ___/8

Count the animals and write down who came to the party.

1 There are three _____.   6 There _____ two _____.

2 There is one _____.   7 _____

3 There are two _____.   8 _____

4 There are three _____.   9 _____

5 There _____ one _____.   10 _____

> Wiederholung von **there is / there are**:
> Du verwendest **there is** …, wenn eine Angabe in der **Einzahl** folgt. (There **is one** lion.)
> Du verwendest **there are** …, wenn eine Angabe in der **Mehrzahl** folgt. (There **are three** foxes.)

3 GRAMMAR What will life be like in 20 years?   ___/5

Write sentences about life in 20 years.

Example:

people – not read – many books: *In twenty years people won't read many books.*

1 people – have – fast and safe cars

   _____

2 students – not have – teachers – have – computers only (2p)

   _____

3 there – be – no more shops in small villages

   _____

4 people – buy – everything – on the internet

   _____

> Um auszudrücken, was in der Zukunft geschehen wird, benutzt du **will + Infinitiv**.
> Es gibt für **alle** Personen nur **eine Form**: I/you/he/she/it/they will …
> Die Kurzform von will ist 'll: I'll, you'll usw.

4 GRAMMAR What Josh will do if he gets a dog:

___ / 6

Finish Josh's sentences.

1. If my parents buy a dog for me, I …
2. I'll call her Lulu if …
3. If the weather is nice, …
4. I'll take Lulu to the animal clinic if …
5. I'll help in the kitchen if …
6. If my friends come to my house, …

1 _____
2 _____
3 _____
4 _____
5 _____
6 _____

☞ **Bedingungssätze Typ 1 (Conditional sentences type 1)**
Die **Bedingung** steht im **if-Satz**, die **Folge** für die Zukunft davon steht im **Hauptsatz**.

if – Satz (Bedingung)	Hauptsatz (Folge für die Zukunft)
simple present	*future oder can, must oder ein Imperativ*
If you **give** a hedgehog water,	it**'ll be** happy.
If you **go** to Bristol Zoo,	you **can watch** many different animals.
If Jack **does** his homework	he **can play** football longer.

Unit 3 | Klassenarbeit A   37

WRITING

___/11

A letter to Ian

You and your friends went to a fun run last week.
Write a letter to your friend Ian in Glasgow and tell him about the fun run. Use the flyer below.

Write

– why you think a fun run is a good idea (2P)

– who or what the fun run was for (1P)

– about your sponsor: Who was it? How did you find him/her?
  How much money did he/she give you for each mile? (3P)

– who you ran with (1P)

– how many miles you ran together (1P)

– what you liked best (2P)

– an end (1P)

You can start like this:

Bristol, 1st June

Dear Ian,
I went to a fun run last week. ...

Animal Helpline Bristol – Fun run for young and old

- Come and join our fun run in Bristol on 23rd May, 9 am – 3 pm.
- Find a sponsor for your miles and run as long as you like.
- Come with all your friends and run 21 miles together.
- Every mile helps an animal.
- The money goes directly to Animal Helpline.

See you on 23rd May!!!

   Denke daran, deinen Brief mit einer Grußformel zu beginnen und zu beenden.
   Denke daran, das **simple past** zu verwenden, da du über ein Ereignis in der Vergangenheit schreibst.
   Achte auf die Formen bei den unregelmäßigen Verben.
   Du kannst sie im Buch auf S. 210 nachschlagen.

Unit 3 — Klassenarbeit B

Gesamtpunktzahl ohne Speaking _____ / 75 Note _____

Gesamtpunktzahl mit Speaking _____ / 85 Note _____

READING _____ / 20

This week in your "KIDS' MAGAZINE": PETS

You are looking for a pet? Here is some information for you about guinea pigs, cats and dogs. It will help you to find the right pet.

HOW TO KEEP YOUR GUINEA PIG HAPPY

Wild guinea pigs live in groups so it's a good idea to keep more than one together. The cage must be big enough so that they can walk around. You can put sawdust[1] on the floor.

It's important to clean the cage every three days. Keep your guinea pigs away from dogs and cats. And don't put the cage in the direct sun. Your guinea pigs want a nice bed, so put some hay[2] into the cage too. Make sure your guinea pigs get enough water: you can put up a bottle in the cage. Your guinea pigs want to run around in your garden. But check that they can't run away. It's best if you buy special guinea pig food.

CATS ARE GOOD TO HAVE

Cats are good pets if they can go outside. Cats love to be in the garden, so it's nice if they can go in and out as they like. But please check that there aren't any dangerous roads.

They like a quiet and warm place, maybe on a sofa. They will sit quietly there and sleep all day. If the weather is good, your cat will lie in a sunny place in your garden. If your cat is hungry, it will walk to its cat bowl. You can buy special cats' food. Your cat must always get enough water. Milk isn't good for your cat.

Sometimes cats are like people: if you do things that your cat doesn't like, it will not be friendly to you. Then it won't look at you for some time. Your cat likes playing. So give it a soft ball to play with, or just a piece of paper or some wool. Your cat likes to play alone.

A DOG CAN BE A GOOD FRIEND

Here are a few ideas to help you and your dog to live together.

The RSPCA say that it costs about £700 a year to look after a dog. Dogs eat different things but they need fresh water every day. Dogs don't want to be alone the whole day and want to run around every day. Let your dog go out in the garden and go for walks with your dog in the park or in the woods as often as you can. So before you buy a dog, you must make sure that you have enough time for your dog every day.

It can be hard work to teach a dog some easy things, but it's good for your dog. You can teach your dog at home or go to dog classes where it can meet other dogs. Your dog will learn to do what you want it to do. Make sure your dog knows its name. This makes teaching easier for you and the dog.

---

[1] sawdust ['sɔːdʌst] *Sägemehl*   [2] hay [heɪ] *Heu*

Unit 3 | Klassenarbeit B   39

1 About the pets   ____ / 7

*Look at the pictures. Draw lines from the pet to the things that are important for the pet.
There are more things than you need.*

2 What do you know about the pets?   ____ / 13

*Use the information from the texts. Tick (✔) the right boxes.
There are **13 correct** answers.*

		guinea pig	cat	dog
1	It's better to have more than one of them.			
2	You must spend a lot of money on this pet in one year.			
3	It likes the garden.			
4	It needs a bed.			
5	It wants to go for a walk with you.			
6	You can teach it.			
7	It likes sleeping.			
8	This pet likes to be alone.			
9	Be friendly to this pet – or it will not be friendly to you.			
10	Don't leave this pet alone the whole day.			
11	This pet doesn't like the sun.			

Unit 3 | Klassenarbeit B

LANGUAGE

/ 43

1 WORDS Find the words. / 10

Find the words and fill them in.

1 The children are playing __ __ __ __ __ __ .
2 Tonight the __ __ __ is beautiful.
3 What a lot of __ __ __ __ __ __ !
4 Sandra is in the __ __ __ __ __ __ __ . Paul is __ __ __ __ __ __ __ her.
5 Liam and Peter want to make a __ __ __ .
6 Last month we __ __ __ __ __ __ to London.
7 Oh __ __ __ ! The window is __ __ __ __ __ __ .
8 Your room must always look __ __ __ a __ __ __ __ __ __ d __ .

*You can make the expression of **three words** with the letters from the boxes if you put them in the right order.*

2 WORDS Say it in English ____/12

Was sagst du, wenn du ...

1   ... jemanden darauf aufmerksam machen möchtest, dass er frieren wird?

    _____

2   ... eine Übung nicht schwierig findest?

    _____

3   ... möchtest, dass jemand etwas aufhebt?

    _____

4   ... jemanden bittest, dir etwas zu erklären?

    _____

5   ... bedauerst, dass du gehen musst?

    _____

6   ... jemanden bittest, das Eis kühl zu halten?

    _____

3 GRAMMAR In the pet shop ____/5

Gillian and her mother are in the pet shop. Gillian wants a pet, but she doesn't know which.
Fill in the correct verb forms.

Mrs Brother   Now Gillian, let's look at all the pets.

Gillian   Well, Mum. If I _____ (take) a dog, I will have to go for a walk every morning.

Mrs Brother   Yes, that's right, dear. But if you get up a bit earlier every morning, this _____ (not be) a problem.

Gillian   Hm, I don't know. What about a cat, Mum?

Mrs Brother   Well, if you buy a cat, things _____ (be) easier.

Gillian   You're right. But what can we do if our cat _____ (run) on the road?

Mrs Brother   Yes, that's another big problem. What about a budgie?

Gillian   OK, Mum. I think I'll have the budgie.

Mrs Brother   If you want a budgie, you _____ (clean) the cage. OK?

Conditional sentences type 1 (Bedingungssätze Typ 1)	
if-Satz	Hauptsatz
simple present	will-future must can Imperativ (Befehl, Aufforderung)

4 GRAMMAR My cat Minky

____ / 12

Last week Amy wrote about her cat Minky.
Complete the text with the correct form of the words in brackets (adjective or adverb).

Minky is a _____ (nice) cat. She sits _____ (quiet) on my bed for hours. But if I don't give her a good lunch, she is _____ (angry) and walks away _____ (quick). She is very _____ (clever), too. If she sees a bird she will move _____ (slow), so that the bird can't see her. When the bird flies away, Minky turns round _____ (angry). Last year she had five _____ (sweet) babies. She fed them _____ (careful). After two months we gave them away to some _____ (good) friends. I was so _____ (sad). But when I saw them play _____ (happy) in my friends' garden it was OK.

> **Besonderheiten in der Bildung von Adverbien:**
> 1 **y** wird zu **i**: angry ▶ angr**i**ly
> 2 **le** wird zu **ly**: terrible ▶ terri**bly**
> 3 Nach **ic** wird **ally** angehängt: fantastic ▶ fantastic**ally**

5 GRAMMAR My dog Norah

____ / 4

*Imagine you have got a dog – Norah. Write **four** sentences about what she does and how she does it.*
*Use the ideas below – use **four** different adverbs and **four** different activities.*

Adverbs:
slowly • quickly • well • quietly • happily • badly • carefully • terribly • fast • …

Ideas for activities:
say hello • run • bark[1] • do tricks • bring the newspaper • follow the neighbours' cat • …

Example:
Norah barks loudly.

1 _____
2 _____
3 _____
4 _____

---

[1] bark [bɑːk] *bellen*

MEDIATION

____/12

Finding out about Animal Helpline

Welcome to Bristol Animal Helpline

Who are we?

We are a big organization for animals. We love animals and we want to stop cruelty to animals[1].

Here in Bristol there are the *Animals Home* and the *Animal Clinic*.

Every year we find new families for thousands of animals, like cats, dogs, rabbits, guinea pigs and birds.

We don't get any money from the government[2]. So money is always a problem. We get our money only from sponsors.

Some people like our work but haven't got any money to give to us. These people work here as volunteers. They come to our *Animals Home* and help us with the animals. If you love animals and are looking for a place to help, then just come to *Animal Helpline*. You will like it! We are a really good team!

Every year in June we have a fun run. We get a lot of money from these fun runs. Last year about 800 people ran more than 4000 miles for us. It was one of our happiest days.

Many people give money to us every month or every year. We even get money from young children. They save some of their pocket money every month and happily give it to us. In the year 2007 an old woman won some money in a lottery. She gave us £1000!

If you want to tell us about cruelty to an animal, please call our helpline.

You found this website on the internet. Your uncle works in a pet shop in Germany and is interested in *Animal Helpline*. He asks you what the website is about.

1. Sag mal, was ist *Animal Helpline*? (2 items)
2. Bekommt diese Organisation Geld von der Regierung oder woher bekommt sie es?
3. Es gibt doch sicherlich viele Leute, die die Arbeit von *Animal Helpline* gut finden, aber nicht so viel Geld haben. Wie können diese Leute *Animal Helpline* unterstützen?
4. Was steht da genau über den Sponsorenlauf? (3 items)
5. Wie können Kinder helfen?
6. Und was steht da über die ältere Frau?
7. Wann soll man die Helpline anrufen?

 Auch wenn du nicht jedes Wort des Textes verstehst, kannst du die Fragen deines Onkels beantworten. Bei manchen Fragen steht 2 oder 3 **items**. Dann musst du 2 oder 3 Fakten zur Beantwortung der Frage beitragen.

---

[1] cruelty to animals ['kruːəlti] *Tierquälerei*   [2] government ['gʌvənmənt] *Regierung*

44 Unit 3 | Klassenarbeit B

SPEAKING   ____ / 10

🎧 09 An interview about pets

The presenter of Bristol Today is interviewing Alan about his pet. Listen to the interview.

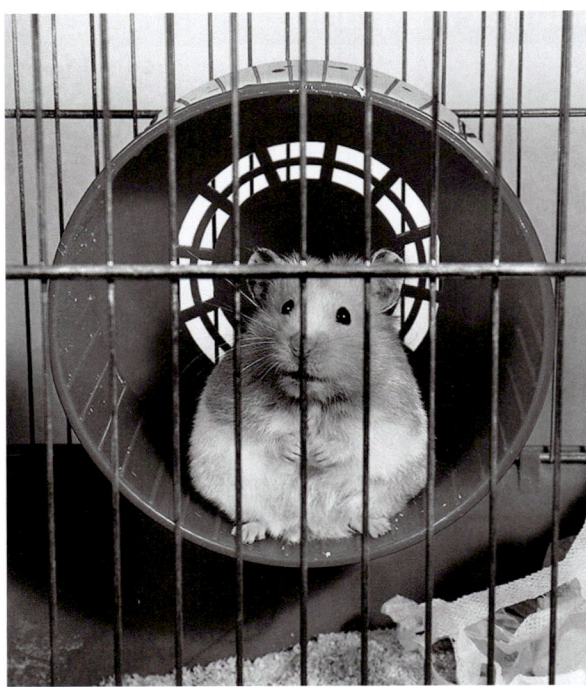

🎧 10 Now you

Now the presenter is interviewing you. First make notes about your pet:

your pet: (1P)	
he/she, name? (1P)	
what's special? (3 items) (3P)	
who feeds / what food? (2P)	
parents: help? (2 items) (2P)	
holidays? (1P)	

Now listen to the speaker's questions and answer them.

Klassenarbeit A

Gesamtpunktzahl _____ / 66   Note _____

READING

_____ / 23

 Es ist oft sinnvoll, die Aufgaben vor dem Text gründlich durchzulesen. Dann weißt du, worauf du beim Lesen des Textes achten musst und du kannst die Aufgaben gleich beim Lesen bearbeiten. Dann siehst du, dass es auch nicht so schlimm ist, wenn du nicht jedes Wort verstehst, weil du die Aufgaben trotzdem lösen kannst.

BBC[1] Wales Bus on tour

The BBC Wales Bus was on tour again last week, when it visited Valley School in Carmarthenshire in Wales. It stopped there for two days. The bus has 20 computers on board where the students can work. They can surf the internet, download pictures and music, work on projects and chat with friends or send them e-mails. But the most interesting part is always the small radio studio on the bus.

Students from Year 5–7 were very excited. They got into groups to visit the big red bus, and worked on different tasks[2].

Year 5 started on Monday morning. Their task was to work on the topic "My way to school". First everybody worked alone to find out about questions like: How far is it to school? Are there any dangerous roads? Must I go by bus or can I walk? Some of the students even made maps[3] on the computer to describe their way to school. Then they reported to the other students. The results were interesting.

On Monday afternoon it was Year 6's turn. They practised presentations because they wanted to get better. They practised with cameras. This was difficult because it was the first time for most students. But they knew how important it is to learn to give better presentations. So they worked hard. Then they watched the films, talked about the presentations and made them better.

Year 7 was on the bus on Tuesday morning. Their task was to prepare a school trip to Cardiff. They surfed the internet for information. One group found out about museums in Cardiff. A second group looked for information about how to get wool[4] from sheep. Group 3 collected ideas for an interesting day trip to Caerphilly Castle with its leaning tower. And the last group found out about the train times and how much a return ticket is.

And on Tuesday afternoon? On Tuesday afternoon the small radio studio was open for all the students. And everybody could ask for their favourite song on the radio. That was great! Everybody had fun on the BBC Wales Bus.

---

[1] BBC = **B**ritish **B**roadcasting **C**orporation *britischer Radio- und Fernsehsender*   [2] task [tɑːsk] *Aufgabe*
[3] map [maep] *(Land-)Karte*   [4] wool [wʊl] *Wolle*

Unit 4 | Klassenarbeit A

1 The BBC Wales Bus and the students

____ / 14

Fill in the chart with the information from the text: one fact for each bullet point •.

	Year 5	Year 6	Year 7	Everybody
When?	• _____	• _____	• _____	• _____
What was their topic?	• _____	• _____	• _____	open for everybody
What did they do?	• _____ • _____	• _____ • _____	• _____ • _____	• _____

2 After the visit to the BBC Bus

____ / 9

After their visit to the BBC Bus the students talked about it. Who said what?
Write the numbers of the statements into the speech bubbles of Megan, David and Abby.

Megan, Year 5

David, Year 6

Abby, Year 7

1 "It was hard to talk in front of the camera."
2 "A group ticket to Cardiff is ..."
3 "When I give a presentation, I'm not nervous now."
4 "I didn't know that it is three miles from my house to school."
5 "I have to be careful when I ride my bike to school."
6 "It was so funny when Mike suddenly laughed and couldn't stop any more."
7 "There are some really nice restaurants in Cardiff where you can get a cheap lunch."
8 "I can read maps[1] now."
9 "The last train back to Cardiff is at 10.30."

[1] map [mæp] *(Land-)Karte*

Unit 4 | Klassenarbeit A 47

LANGUAGE

____/29

1 GRAMMAR What have they just done?

____/7

a) *Look at the notes. Write down what they have just done.*

1 Caroline – write an e-mail

_____

2 Jenny and Anna – find information about Caerphilly Castle

_____

3 Martin – look at the timetable

_____

4 Sue – read about a museum in Cardiff

_____

b) *Now you*

What have you already done today? / What haven't you done yet?
Write at least **three** sentences and use the present perfect.

>   Denke daran, für das **present perfect** have/has + die dritte Form zu verwenden.
> Bei unregelmäßigen Verben ist die dritte Form natürlich auch unregelmäßig: eat – ate – eaten.

2 WORDS Describing a picture

____/10

a) *Look at the picture and write down the words.*   (4 P)

1 _____
2 _____
3 _____
4 _____
5 _____
6 _____
7 _____
8 _____

b) *Now describe the picture in complete sentences. Start with the foreground and then go to the background. Find a topic sentence (= einleitender Satz) for your text.*   (6 P)

>   Wichtige Hinweise zu **nützlichen Wörtern** und zur richtigen **Verwendung der Zeiten** bei **Bildbeschreibungen** findest du im Klassenarbeitstrainer auf S. 11.
> Hilfen, wie du einen **topic sentence** formulieren kannst, findest du im **Skills File** in deinem Englischbuch auf S. 129.

3 WORDS Opposites[1]

___/6

a) Find the opposites of these words:

1 husband ◄► _____   4 quiet ◄► _____

2 strong ◄► _____   5 valley ◄► _____

3 dirty ◄► _____   6 exciting ◄► _____

b) Find three more opposites:

1 _____ ◄► _____

2 _____ ◄► _____

3 _____ ◄► _____

4 STUDY SKILLS How to give a good presentation

___/6

Here are three paragraphs:

a) Put the sentences of each paragraph (♣ ♦ ♠) in the right order. Write the letters next to the numbers.

♣
- A You should only have a few key words on your cards.
- B First you must say what you are talking about.
- C Then start with your information.
- D Don't read out your text.

1 ☐   2 ☐   3 ☐   4 ☐

♦
- A Then wait till everybody is quiet.
- B Before you start talking, prepare everything you need.
- C A good presentation needs good preparation[2].
- D Hang up posters, get the projector ready.

1 ☐   2 ☐   3 ☐   4 ☐

♠
- A Then ask for questions.
- B When you show pictures, you must always explain them.
- C At the end of the presentation you should say that you have finished.
- D Look at your listeners as often as you can.

1 ☐   2 ☐   3 ☐   4 ☐

b) Find the first, the second and the third paragraph. The topic sentence helps you to find the first paragraph.

♣ = ☐   ♦ = ☐   ♠ = ☐

---

[1] opposites ['ɒpəsɪts] Gegensatzpaare   [2] preparation [prepə'reɪʃn] Vorbereitung

Unit 4 | Klassenarbeit A

MEDIATION

____ / 14

Where can we go?

You are staying at a camping site¹ in Wales together with your parents. You and your parents want to plan some day trips. So you go to the tourist information centre to get some information. Because your parents don't speak very much Welsh or English you help with the conversation.

Your mum	Sag ihr bitte, dass wir hier auf dem Campingplatz wohnen und gerne einige Tagesausflüge planen möchten. Frag sie dann bitte, ob sie uns ein paar Tipps geben kann.
You	Good morning. We are staying _____
You	_____
Woman	Yes, of course. There are many things to do here. But first let me ask you: Do you want to visit museums or do you want to go to our famous beaches?
You	Sie sagt, dass _____
You	_____
Your mum	Das ist schwierig zu beantworten. Wenn die Sonne scheint und es warm ist, gehen wir an die Strände. Aber wir brauchen auch Ideen für schlechtes Wetter. Wir könnten in ein oder zwei Museen gehen, finde ich.
You	_____
You	_____
Woman	OK. I understand. On this map here you can see all the beaches near the camping site. I mark these two nice beaches for you on the map. You will like them.
You	Also, auf dieser Karte _____
You	_____
Woman	Now, if the weather is bad, there are many small museums. Here is a brochure with all the information.
You	_____
You	_____
Your mum	Das sind ja tolle Ideen. Bedank dich bitte und frag noch gleich nach einem guten Café.
You	_____
Woman	Yes, you can go to the Red Dragon. That's very good. Bye-bye and have nice trips.
Your mum	Also, das habe ich jetzt auch verstanden. Thank you very much and bye-bye.

¹ camping site ['kæmpɪŋ saɪt] *Campingplatz*

Unit 4 — Klassenarbeit B

Gesamtpunktzahl ohne Speaking _____ / 70 Note _____

Gesamtpunktzahl mit Speaking _____ / 85 Note _____

LISTENING

_____ / 22

🎧 11 **Three reports on an accident**

There has been an accident. The police talk to a boy, a woman and a man. Listen to what they say.

New word
light [laɪt] *Licht*

1 About the accident _____ / 6

Listen and match the photos to the information. Draw lines.

boy  has a shock

woman  called the police

man  was a bit late

2 More facts about the accident ____ / 16

Read the chart first. Then listen again and find the different facts.

	The boy's story	The woman's story	The man's story
lights on the boy's bike: yes/no?			
the boy's bike: slow/fast?			
the boy's clothes			
the woman's car: fast/slow?			
the boy's injuries[1]		✗	
Who called the paramedics?	✗		

LANGUAGE ____ / 35

1 WORDS irregular verbs ____ / 10

Fill in the missing forms.

Infinitive	Simple past form	Past participle	German translation
(to) be			
(to) eat			
(to) find			
(to) go			
(to) come			
(to) have			
(to) take			
(to) make			
(to) do			
(to) see			

[1] injury ['ɪndʒəri] *Verletzung*

Unit 4 | Klassenarbeit B

2 GRAMMAR After the accident   ___/9

An accident has just happened in Leicester Road. Read the notes and write down what the people have done or haven't done yet. Write one sentence for each note. Be careful where you put the words **already**, **yet**, **just** (siehe Hinweisbox).

1 Alan – phone – the police   **already**

_____

2 the paramedics – take the boy – to hospital   **just**

_____

3 two policemen – talk to – the man   **already**

_____

4 the policemen – not write – the report   **yet**

_____

5 the driver of the car – not visit – the boy in hospital   **yet**

_____

6 the policemen – phone – the boy's parents   **just**

_____

  Die **Bildung des present perfect** kannst du dir in Erinnerung rufen, wenn du dir den Lerntipp **The present perfect trip** auf S. 29 im Lösungseinleger deines Klassenarbeitstrainer anschaust.

already = schon, **not ... yet** = noch nicht, **just** = gerade eben
Solche Adverbien der unbestimmten Zeit findest du oft in *present perfect*-Sätzen.
Sie stehen in der Regel direkt vor dem past participle: *I've **already** parked the car.*
Ausnahme: *yet* steht am Satzende: *I haven't seen Dan **yet**.*

3 WORDS At the doctor's   ___/6

The following people are sitting in Dr Smith's waitingroom. Everybody has a different problem. Write what's wrong with them.

1 Mr Miller has _____.

2 John _____.

3 Sally _____.

4 Mr Baker _____.

5 Susan _____.

6 Mrs Marple _____.

4 GRAMMAR Mum and Dad have got a lot of questions

___ / 5

When the boy's parents visit him in hospital they have got a lot of questions.
Form the questions and write them down.

1 you — phone Grandma
2 the driver of the car — read the new book
3 the doctor — write you an e-mail
4 your teacher — see you
5 your friends — visit you
6 you — bring you the homework

1 Have you phoned Grandma?

2 _____

3 _____

4 _____

5 _____

6 _____

5 GRAMMAR Where will they be when?

___ / 5

Write sentences where the boys and girls will be when. Think of place before time.

Ort vor Zeit

Natale – next Monday

Isabel – tomorrow

Barry – next weekend

Tracy and Terry – in the afternoon

Adam – in a few minutes

1 Natale will be _____.

2 _____

3 _____

4 _____

5 _____

WRITING

____ / 13

Mike's letter to his grandma

*Mike is in hospital after his accident. He is writing a letter to his grandma.
He writes about:*

– when and where the accident was
– what happened
– the paramedics
– what's wrong with him and how he feels
– what it is like in hospital
– how long he must stay in hospital
– who visits him and what they bring
– when he can go home from hospital

Write a beginning and an ending.

> **In dieser Schreibübung musst du verschiedene Zeiten verwenden**
>
> Überlege daher vorher:
> - Hat das, worüber ich schreiben will, in der Vergangenheit stattgefunden
>   ▶ **simple past** *(Last Wednesday I went ...)*
> - Beschreibt das, worüber ich schreiben will, einen momentanen Zustand oder findet es regelmäßig statt?
>   ▶ **simple present** *(I have a terrible headache. / My parents visit me every day.)*
> - Findet das, worüber ich schreiben will, erst in der Zukunft statt
>   ▶ **will-future** *(I will go home tomorrow).*

SPEAKING

____ / 15

🎧 12 School paramedics

Manuel is an exchange student from Essen, Germany. At his school in Germany he is a school paramedic. He explains what school paramedics at his school do. Listen to Manuel.

🎧 13 Now you

*Bessy wants to do an interview with Manuel for the school radio. Imagine you are Manuel and answer Bessy's questions.
Listen to Bessy's questions and use the pictures for your answers.*

> - Höre dir Bessys Fragen zuerst einmal an. Schaue dir dazu die Bilder an.
>   Erinnere dich daran, was Manuel über seine Aufgabe als Schulsanitäter berichtet hat.
>   Überlege, wie du die Fragen beantworten kannst.
> - Höre dir dann die Fragen ein zweites Mal an und beantworte sie.
>   Drücke dabei die Pausentaste, damit du Zeit für deine Antworten hast.

Year 7–9

Tuesday afternoon – six weeks –
told about work, what they can/can't do

hurt students – sometimes call Essen paramedics

Bessy Who are the new school paramedics and what years are they from?

You ...

Bessy Who did the training with you?

You ...

Bessy When was the training and what did you learn?

You ...

Bessy How can the school paramedics help?

You ...

Bessy When and where can students find you?

You ...

Klassenarbeit A

Gesamtpunktzahl _____ / 65   Note _____

_____ / 17

LISTENING

 14   **A great team: the "Shocking Smoothies"**

The Cotham School kids are talking about the BigBanana juice bar and they have got an idea. Listen to Alex, Julie, Kerry and Ralph.

New word
head teacher [ˌhed ˈtiːtʃə] *Schulleiter/in*

☞ Lies dir vor dem Hören die Aufgabe genau durch. Dann weißt du, worauf du beim Hören achten musst und du wirst feststellen, dass du die Aufgaben lösen kannst, auch wenn du nicht jedes Wort verstehst.

1   Smoothies at school

_____ / 8

*Look at the pictures. Listen to the text. You must tick (✔) **eight** things that the kids are talking about.*

2   More about the smoothies bar

_____ / 9

Read the following statements. Then listen again and tick (✔) the correct box.

		Right	Wrong
1	Alex liked the strawberry smoothie in the bar.		
2	They want to go to the bar again tomorrow afternoon.		
3	Kerry thinks that smoothies at school are too difficult.		
4	They don't need to ask the head teacher.		
5	They want to give all the money to Animal Helpline.		
6	They already know the price for one smoothie.		
7	The Smoothies team must clean the dirty glasses.		
8	They want to hang up posters.		
9	They can't find a name for their bar.		

Unit 5 | Klassenarbeit A 57

LANGUAGE

____/ 33

1 GETTING BY IN ENGLISH Say it in English

____/ 8

Was sagst du, wenn ...

1 du jemanden darauf aufmerksam machen möchtest, dass er/sie in die falsche Richtung geht?
   _____

2 du denkst, dass jemand etwas nicht ernst meint oder Witze macht?
   _____

3 dein Mitspieler ein Feld zurückgehen soll?
   _____

4 du wissen willst, wer dran ist?
   _____

5 du möchtest, dass jemand kurz warten soll?
   _____

6 du jemanden bittest, auf deinen Hund aufzupassen?
   _____

7 du ein Lied ziemlich gut findest?
   _____

8 du herausfinden willst, ob jemand weiß, wem dieser Geldbeutel gehört?
   _____

2 WORDS Plural of nouns

____/ 5

Write down the plural of the nouns.

1 one dice   two _____   6   one man   two _____

2 one strawberry   two _____   7   one woman   two _____

3 one waitress   two _____   8   one child   two _____

4 one thief   two _____   9   one deer   two _____

5 one wife   two _____   10 one sheep   two _____

3 GRAMMAR What are they going to do? ____ / 12

Look at the team plan for the „Shocking Smoothies Bar". Sometimes they have changed[1] their plan.
So write what everybody is or is not going to do.

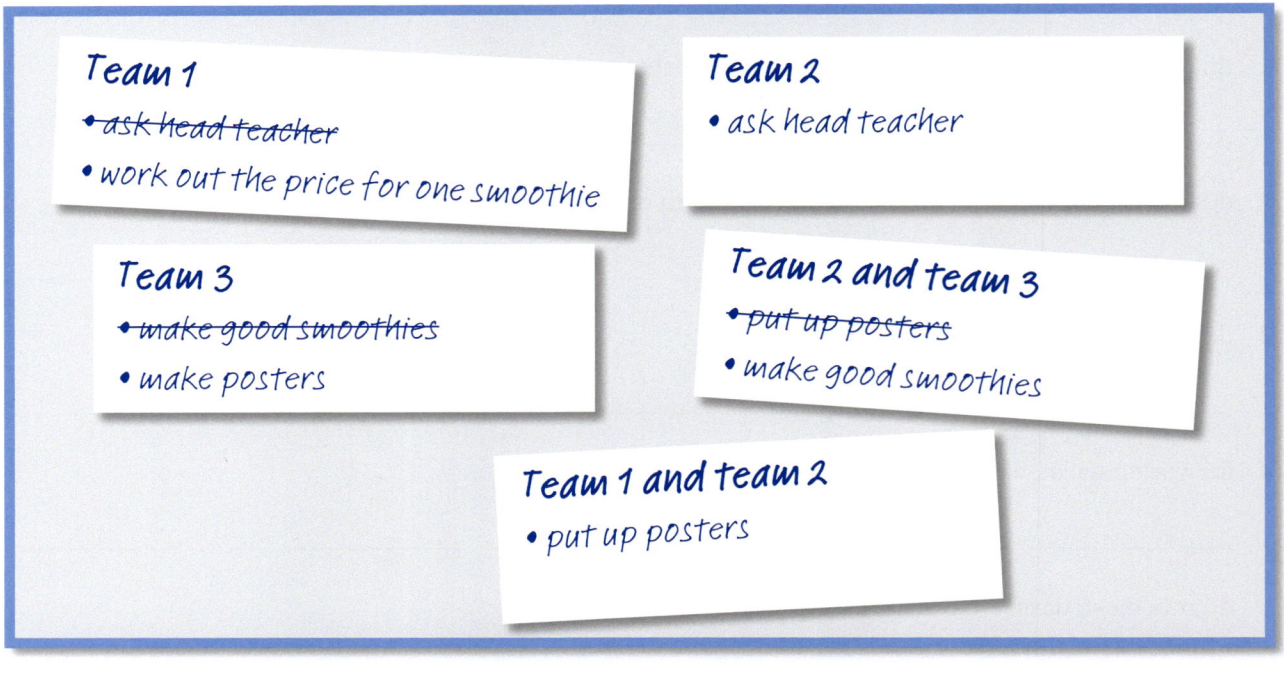

1 Team 1 isn't going _____.

2 It's going to _____.

3 Team 2 _____.

4 Team 3 _____.

5 It's _____.

6 Team 2 and team 3 _____.

7 They are _____.

8 Team 1 and team 2 _____.

Now you

Write what you are going to do this afternoon / tomorrow morning / next Saturday.
Write at least **three** sentences.

1 _____

2 _____

3 _____

> Im **Grammar File 12** im Englischbuch auf S. 145 kannst du nachschlagen, wie man das **going to-future** bildet.

[1] (to) change   [tʃeɪndʒ]   ändern

Unit 5 | Klassenarbeit A

4 STUDY SKILLS New attraction: Healthy but good

_____/8

You have read an article on the website of Cotham School about their smoothies bar.
Your friends are asking you about this attraction: Read your friends' questions:

1. What's special about the smoothies?
2. Are the smoothies expensive?
3. When do they sell the smoothies?
4. Does their head teacher like your idea?

First find the four facts in the text for your answers and mark them. Then answer the questions in sentences.

Cotham School

Healthy but good
New attraction at Cotham School in Bristol

A group of students of Cotham School has just worked out a new attraction: everybody can get healthy and delicious smoothies at lunch break now. The Smoothies Team makes the smoothies and sells them at a cheap price. They are going to give some of the money to the Animal Helpline and spend the rest on the next school trip. The head teacher thinks that the idea shows good teamwork. "We got the idea when we tried the delicious smoothies in a juice bar. We understood that good food can be healthy too," says Sophie, one of the Smoothies team.

WRITING

_____/17

An e-mail to the Shocking Smoothies Team

You have read an article on the website of Cotham School about their smoothies bar. You like the idea and want to find out more about the smoothies project, because you and your friends want to open a smoothies bar at your school too.

Write an e-mail to the Shocking Smoothies team and ask for details. The notes will help you.
Don't forget to write a beginning and an ending.

e-mail to Cotham School:
- read article on the internet
- like your idea
- open smoothies bar at our school
- many questions
- how – start?
- students – how many?
- price?
- problems?
- ask head teacher – before you started?
- glasses?
- send – recipe

 Fragen mit do/does/did:
Do you read many books?
Does John like cake?
Did you go to the milk bar yesterday?
How often do you go to the swimming pool?

**Denke auch an folgende Möglichkeiten
Fragen zu beginnen:**
What about …?
Could you …?
How much/many …?

[1] recipe ['resəpi] *Rezept*

Unit 5 — Klassenarbeit B

Gesamtpunktzahl ohne Speaking _____ / 60 Note _____

Gesamtpunktzahl mit Speaking _____ / 70 Note _____

READING _____/12

New games for everybody

Last week was very exciting for the students of 6 PF. Mr Fisher divided the class into eight teams. Every team had to invent[1] a new board game. A difficult task!

First the children brought their board games from home. The teams found out how you play the different games and played them. So they learned how you must write the instructions for a board game. They also talked about what colours you must use so that the games look interesting and exciting.

Every team found a special topic for their game. Then they started to make their game. It was a lot of work and every student in the team had a job. They drew their game, then some coloured the board, some made nice counters and dice and all the other things that they needed for their games. They needed a lot of glue, scissors and paper. The instructions were the most difficult job. You must write them clearly so that every player understands the game. In the end they even made a box for their game, painted it and wrote the name on top.

After many hours of work the games were ready. The games had all different names, sometimes they were funny too. Here are some of the names: *At the Zoo, Up and down High Street, Isidor and the Market, The Great Harbour Game, Asterix and Obelix* and *A Funny Tour around the School*.

When all the games were ready, they played all of them because they wanted to find "The best game of 6 PF". It was difficult because all the games were good. So they had to look at the colours of the game, the instructions and if the game was exciting. In the end "The Great Harbour Game" with all its colourful ships was the winner. Congratulations!

1 Headings _____/5

Here are five headings. Match the headings and the five paragraphs. Draw lines.

paragraph 1   a) Lots of interesting games

paragraph 2   b) Finding the super game

paragraph 3   c) Making groups

paragraph 4   d) Making a new game

paragraph 5   e) Playing games from home

---

[1] (to) invent [ɪnˈvent] *erfinden*

2 About the week of the games

____/7

Read the sentences. Then tick (✔) the correct box.

		Right	Wrong	Not in the text
1	The students of 6PF invented a new game together.	☐	☐	☐
2	Every team got a topic from Mr Fisher.	☐	☐	☐
3	Everybody in the team had a job.	☐	☐	☐
4	At the beginning some teams had problems.	☐	☐	☐
5	They also made coloured boxes.	☐	☐	☐
6	The instructions of the games weren't clear.	☐	☐	☐
7	The students of the best game got a present.	☐	☐	☐

LANGUAGE

____/31

1 WORDS Find the words.

____/9

Find the words and fill them in.

1 Smoothies are good and   _ _ _ _ _ _ _ .
2 You need this to play a board game: _ _ _ _ .
3 There are three sizes: small, medium and   _ _ _ _ _ .
4 You are buying something in a shop – you are a   _ _ _ _ _ _ _ .
5 He brings your coffee in a café: _ _ _ _ _ _ .
6 The smoothie is super. It's   _ _ _ _ _ _ _ _ .
7 The opposite of leave is: _ _ _ _ _ _ .
8 You open the door with a   _ _ _ .

Now you

Can you explain the word from the boxes?

 is when _____

_____

Unit 5 | Klassenarbeit B

2 GRAMMAR Plans for the game ___/5

*Mr Fisher is asking the different teams about their games. Write down his questions with **going to**.*

 Fragen mit going to:

Mit Fragewort: What are you going to do next?
Ohne Fragewort: Is he going to sing another song?

1 you – make – a game about animals
2 Peter – work on – the instructions
3 you – help – John with the counters
4 you ~~make~~ – a box for your game
5 when – you – show – the game – to the class

1 _____
2 _____
3 _____
4 _____
5 _____

3 WORDS The Great Harbour Game ___/7

*While¹ the teams are making their games they are talking a lot about the game.
Complete their dialogue with:*

| some • any • something • somewhere • somebody • anywhere • anybody |

 some und die mit **some** zusammengesetzten Wörter stehen vor allem in bejahten Sätzen.
any und die mit **any** zusammengesetzen Wörter stehen vor allem in verneinten Sätzen und Fragen.

Sue   I need _____ help. Can _____ help me please?

Mike OK. How can I help?

Sue   Well, I'm drawing the board. I haven't got _____ good ideas for the pictures.

Mike What about pirates?

Sue   That's a good idea.

¹ while [waɪl] *während*

Liz   I can't find our ideas for the instructions. They must be _____.

Sue   I've already looked for them and I couldn't see them _____.

Mike Oh, come on girls, _____ must have them.

Phil Here they are. Jill and I have added _____.

4 GRAMMAR Are the games ready?   ____/4

Look at the list. Say what the students have done or haven't done for their games.

```
all the students   learn how to write the instructions for a game  ✓
Sue                paint the board  ✗
Phil               write the instructions  ✗
Mike and Jill      make six counters  ✓
Liz                paint the box and write the name on it  ✓
```

Example: *All the students have learned how to write the instructions for the game.*

1 _____

2 _____

3 _____

4 _____

5 GRAMMAR How they worked   ____/6

Write how they worked in their teams. Fill in the missing adverbs of manner.

John read the instructions of the game _____ (quick).

The teams worked on their games very _____ (hard).

Tim and Sandra talked about the game _____ (quiet).

The team presented their game _____ (proud).

Now you

Think of what you did yesterday. Then write two sentences how you did it.
Use adjectives from the box as adverbs of manner

```
slow • angry • terrible • good • fast • nice • rude
```

1 _____

2 _____

MEDIATION

____/17

A new game: The terrible red dragon

The terrible red dragon

Number of players:	3 – 5
Age:	10 – 99 years
Time:	about 40 minutes
You need:	a dice, a counter for each player, the board and twelve boxes of gold, the red dragon
Idea of the game:	In a castle a hungry dragon is waiting to eat the players. The players are in the castle because they want to find as much gold as possible. The way through the castle is long and dangerous.
How to start:	Put the counters to the start position. The terrible dragon looks at them. The youngest player throws the dice first. If he/she throws a four he/she can start.
The spaces:	If you land on a brown space you miss a turn. If you land on a golden space you throw again and collect one box of gold. If you land on a black space the dragon moves one space nearer. If you land on a red space you must pay one box of gold to the dragon.
The dragon:	If the dragon lands on your counter it will eat you.
The winner:	If you get to the top of the castle and if you have the most boxes of gold you are the winner.

Your sister got a new game for her birthday. The instructions are in English. You help her. Explain how to play the game.

Erkläre deiner Schwester:

1 wie viele Spieler in welchem Alter mitspielen können   (1P)
2 was man alles zum Spiel benötigt   (3P)
3 die Idee des Spiels   (3P)
4 wie man beginnt   (2P)
5 die Bedeutung der verschiedenen Felder   (4P)
6 die Rolle des Drachens   (2P)
7 wann man gewonnen hat   (2P)

Unit 5 | Klassenarbeit B

SPEAKING

___/ 10

🎧 15 **Let's present our new game**

The students of Form 6 PF have invented new games. Now all teams present their game to the class. Listen to the first team.

> **New word**
> board [bɔːd] *Spielbrett*

Now you

You worked in one of the other teams. Now you present your game to the class.
You can choose a name from the box or think of a new name.

> At the Zoo • Up and down High Street • A Funny Tour around the School • The Great Animal Party • The Round Britain Game • …

Make notes of what you are going to say before you speak.

You must talk about:	Your ideas:
name of the game (1P)	
who was on your team? (1P)	
how many players? how old? (1P)	
what you need for the game (1P)	
idea of the game (2P)	
what is special (red space, green space, questions, …)? (2P)	
who is the winner? (2P)	

Unit 6 — Klassenarbeit A

Gesamtpunktzahl ohne Speaking _____ / 55 Note _____

Gesamtpunktzahl mit Speaking _____ / 70 Note _____

READING _____ / 14

> Oft geht es bei Reading-Aufgaben darum, einen Text gezielt nach Informationen abzusuchen **(Scanning)**. Deshalb ist es sehr wichtig, dass du zunächst die Aufgabe durchliest. Dann kannst du ganz gezielt nach den gefragten Informationen suchen und brauchst nur dort genauer nachlesen, wo du sie findest.

BATH – Daily News Wednesday, 15th July

Visitors in Bath

It's summertime – and this means that there are lots of visitors in Bath. Our reporter Helen Fields talked to some of them yesterday afternoon.

First time

Hello, my name is Philip Smith and this is my wife. Well, we are just here for the day. At the moment we are on holiday. But we decided to stay at home and just go on day trips. So the holidays are not so expensive because we can sleep at home in Gloucester. Yesterday we went to Wales and today we visited the Roman Baths. It's our first time here in Bath and we like it very much. We want to come again and visit the Museum of Costume.

A bike ride to Bath

I'm Susan from Bristol. I'm here with my mum because we want to do some shopping. Yes, I'm on holiday at the moment, well, there is no school, so today we cycled to Bath. It's quite easy to cycle from Bristol to Bath. We've been here lots of times before: we have visited the Roman Baths and the William Herschel Museum. Today we are only going shopping and then cycling home. But at the weekend my parents and I want to visit the Museum of Costume.

Romans in Bath and Heitersheim, Germany

My name is Helen Günter and I am from Germany. I'm on holiday with my two daughters Anna and Lea. Yesterday we flew from Stuttgart to London and then we went to Bath by train. I came to Bath when I was about 15 years old. Now I want to show the Roman Baths to my daughters. You see, there is an old Roman villa in Heitersheim, the town in Germany where we come from, so the girls really wanted to see the Roman Baths here in Bath. This evening we will take the train to Scotland.

Learning English

Hola, I'm José. I'm Spanish and I come from Madrid. I'm here for three weeks and I'm learning English at a language school in Bath. We are 20 students from all over the world. We have lessons in the morning and in the afternoon. But Wednesday afternoon is free. Last Wednesday we went to London. This afternoon my friends and I want to visit the Roman Baths. For next Wednesday we're planning to visit Bristol. No, I've never been to Bath before.

Unit 6 | Klassenarbeit A

Find out about the different visitors ___ / 14

Take notes of all the information about the different people.

	Philip Smith	Helen Günter	Susan	José
where from?				
in Bath alone / together with?				
how long in Bath?				
in Bath for the first time[1]?				
activities in the past this week				
activities today				
activities in the next days				

LANGUAGE ___ / 29

1 WORDS In the city ___ / 10

a) *Think of buildings and places in the city. Find at least ten. Be careful with your spelling. (5P)*

1 _____ 6 _____

2 _____ 7 _____

3 _____ 8 _____

4 _____ 9 _____

5 _____ 10 _____

[1] for the first time *zum ersten Mal*

Unit 6 | Klassenarbeit A

b) *What do you say when you want to tell somebody the way? (5P)*

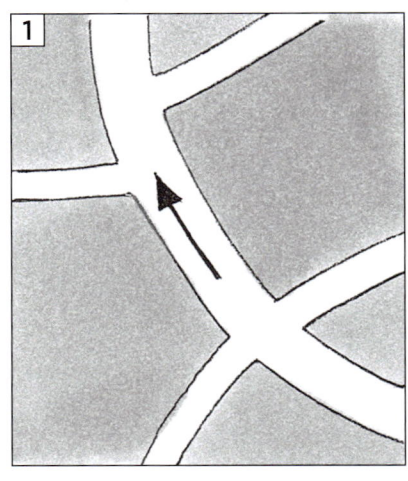 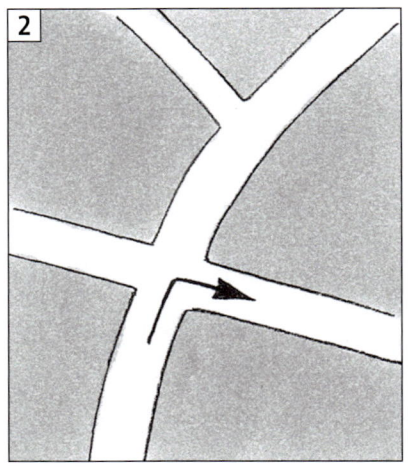 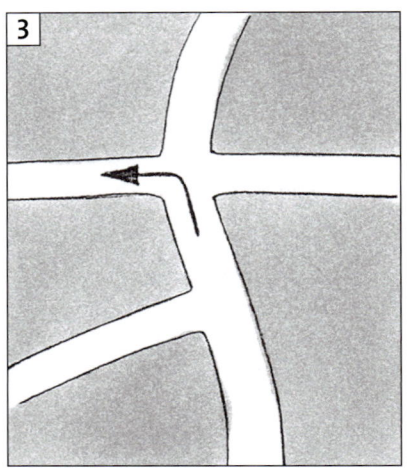

1 _____   2 _____   3 _____

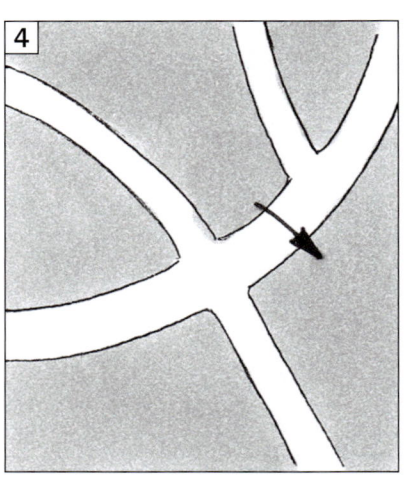 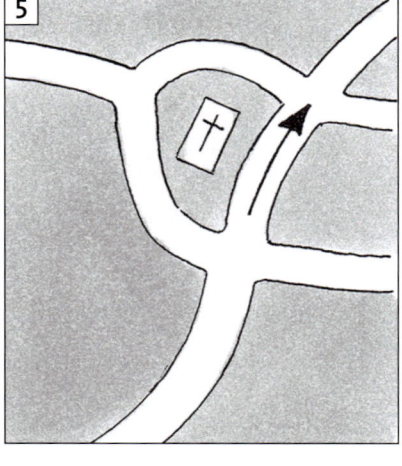

4 _____   5 _____

2   WORDS Find the words.   ____ /7

Find the words and fill them in.

1   One hundred years are a   _ _ _ ■ _ _ .

2   If you have a room with a   _ ■ _ ■ _ _ you can see out.

3   When you are very tired, you must often   _ ■ _ _ .

4   You can go there to have lunch or dinner: _ _ _ _ _ _ _ ■ _ .

5   In Britain the school year has three   _ ■ _ _ _ .

6   At the end of a play, people sometimes   _ _ ■ _ _ loudly.

7   If you put the letters in the boxes in the right order you get a word for the people who watch a play.

■ ■ ■ ■ ■ ■ ■

3 WORDS About the tourists in Bath   /6

Underline the correct prepositions.

1 Susan and her mother are sitting **on/off/at** a table in a café.
2 They will cycle back **for/to/after** Bristol.
3 José wants to have a look **to/for/at** the Roman Baths too.
4 **At/On/In** 5 o'clock he wants to visit the Roman Baths with his friends.
5 Many visitors want to see the old costumes **in/at/by** the Museum of Costumes.
6 **On/At/Off** Wednesdays it is open until 10 pm.

4 GRAMMAR What are they doing?   /6

Write down what the people in the picture are doing.
These verbs will help you. There are two more than you need.

write • visit • sit • ask • learn • go shopping • wait • play

1 Mr and Mrs Smith _____.

2 A girl _____.

3 Susan and her mother _____.

4 Mrs Günter and her daughters _____.

5 José _____.

6 A woman _____.

> **Present progressive:**
>
> **So wird es gebildet:**
>
> I am
> you/they/we are   + **ing**-Form: I am writing a letter.
> he/she/it is   We are playing football.
>   He is reading a book.
>
> **So wird es verwendet:**
>
> Das **Present progressive** wird verwendet, wenn man ausdrücken will, dass etwas gerade geschieht.

Unit 6 | Klassenarbeit A

MEDIATION
___/12

Get to know Bath – Come and enjoy our bus tours

Why not go sightseeing in Bath by bus? It's the easiest way to see our beautiful city. The tour takes about one hour.

There is a lot you can see:
No visit in Bath without going to the Roman Baths!
You will also see the oldest house in Bath (from 1483), the Museum of Costume, the William Herschel House, our famous Royal Victoria Park and the Circus – a round road.

You can start the tour at all the stops. Just look at the map, you'll find every stop there.

If you want to visit one of our museums or have a look at the park, just get off and get on the next bus again. There is a guide on every bus who will explain everything to you and answer all your questions.

Hours
First bus leaves at 9.30 am, last bus at 5 pm.
1st April to 30th November: sightseeing buses run every day.
1st December to 31st March: sightseeing buses run at the weekends only.

You can get off at every stop, visit the museum or the park and then get on the bus again.

More information:
Prices:
Adults: £ 5.99
or: £ 11 (including ticket for Roman Baths)
Children 5–14: £ 2.99
or: £ 8 (including ticket for Roman Baths)
Children under 5: free
Family tickets: £ 15
or: £ 30 (including ticket for Roman Baths)
Tickets:
Get them online at our website or at the Tourist Information in Bath.

Deine Familie möchte Bath besuchen. Du liest diesen Werbetext. Beantworte die Fragen deines Vaters.

Vater Diese Tour sieht sehr interessant aus. Wie lange dauert sie?

Du _____

Vater Ist das so eine Besichtigungstour, auf der man alles von einem Tonband erklärt bekommt? Das finde ich nämlich nicht so gut.

Du _____

Vater Das ist gut. Steht da, was man alles besichtigen kann?

Du _____

Vater Kann man denn auch in den Zirkus gehen oder was soll das bedeuten?

Du _____

Vater Die englischen Parks gefallen mir gut. Kann man sich da auch aufhalten oder muss man immer bei der Gruppe bleiben?

→

Unit 6 | Klassenarbeit A

Du _____

_____

Vater Jetzt noch zu den Preisen: Wir sind ja 2 Erwachsene und zwei Kinder. Sara ist 6 und Peter, du bist 13. Was ist da am preiswertesten?

Du _____

_____

Vater Dann nehmen wir das mit dem Eintritt für die Roman Baths, denn die wollen wir ja unbedingt besichtigen. Wo können wir die Tickets kaufen?

Du _____

SPEAKING

____/15

🎧 16 Learn English in Bath!

Today a reporter is visiting Bath Language School. She interviews some of the students there. Listen to the interviewer's questions and José's answers.

🎧 17 Now you

Now the reporter interviews Julian from Germany. Take his role.

First listen to the reporter's questions again and then collect some ideas.
The information card about Julian can help you. Then answer the reporter's questions.

> ☞ - Im Englischen klingt es eher unfreundlich, wenn man Fragen nur mit einem Wort beantwortet.
> - Achte darauf, wo möglich, **short answers** (= Yes, it is. / No, it isn't. / Yes, I do. / No, I don't. Yes, I have. / No, I haven't) zu benutzen.
> - Reichere deine Antworten mit echten Informationen an, um das Gespräch lebendiger zu machen.
>
> Beispiel: Do you like Bath?
> 1 Yes. (klingt unfreundlich)
> 2 Yes, I do. Bath is a nice town. There are lots of interesting museums. And the Roman Baths are amazing. I went there yesterday. (klingt freundlicher)

BATH LANGUAGE SCHOOL   Student information card

Age: 16
Hometown: Leipzig
Information:
- writes well but finds it difficult to speak English
- thinks school is OK
- has met new friends at school
- is really happy with his host family[1] (one son / 16 years)
- thinks Bath is a nice town
- goes to too many discos!!!

---

[1] host family [haʊst] *Gastfamilie*

Unit 6 — Klassenarbeit B

Gesamtpunktzahl _____ / 55   Note _____

LISTENING

_____ / 11

 A birthday party at the Roman Baths

It's Sara's birthday. Her parents have booked a birthday party at the Roman Baths for Sara and her friends. Matthew from the Roman Baths has prepared the party for them. Listen to Matthew, Sara and Benny.

New word
Latin ['lætɪn] *lateinisch*

☞ Erinnere dich daran, dass du es leichter hast, wenn du dir vor dem Hören die Aufgaben genau durchliest. Dann weißt du, auf was du beim Hören achten musst.

1 Sara's Roman birthday

_____ / 3

Look at the pictures and write down the numbers of the pictures that you can hear something about in the text.

Numbers of the pictures: ☐ ☐ ☐

2 All about the party

_____ / 8

Listen to the text again. Then tick (✔) the right box.

		Right	Wrong
1	They will go swimming.	☐	☐
2	They will get something to eat and to drink at the Roman Baths.	☐	☐
3	Sara and her friends will find out more about how the Romans lived.	☐	☐
4	They can choose one activity.	☐	☐
5	It's easy for Sara to choose the most interesting activity.	☐	☐
6	Sara's friends want to look for things in the sand.	☐	☐
7	Matthew teaches them some Latin words.	☐	☐
8	At the end of the party every child has got a pair of Roman sandals.	☐	☐

Unit 6 | Klassenarbeit B

LANGUAGE

___/27

1 WORDS Word building

___/11

a) *Which words go together? Draw lines. Then write down the words that you found. (5P)*

Zusammensetzungen, bei denen die Wörter getrennt bleiben		Zusammensetzungen, bei denen die Wörter zusammengeschrieben werden	
post	store	care	pecker
police	centre	grand	ache
department	money	sweet	father
leisure	station	head	heart
pocket	office	wood	taker

1 _____ 6 _____

2 _____ 7 _____

3 _____ 8 _____

4 _____ 9 _____

5 _____ 10 _____

b) *) Find the correct words. (6P)*

every   end   body   build

        er   ment   week

              play   inform

                                          ing

    ation

              depart

1 _____ 4 _____

2 _____ 5 _____

3 _____ 6 _____

Unit 6 | Klassenarbeit B

2 WORDS Can you tell me the way? ___/7

Look at the map and explain the way.

	German	English
☞	Biegen Sie rechts in **die** Königstraße.	Turn right into ~~the~~ King Street.
	Im Deutschen setzen wir einen Artikel vor den Straßennamen.	Im Englischen folgt auf die Präposition direkt der Straßenname ohne Artikel.

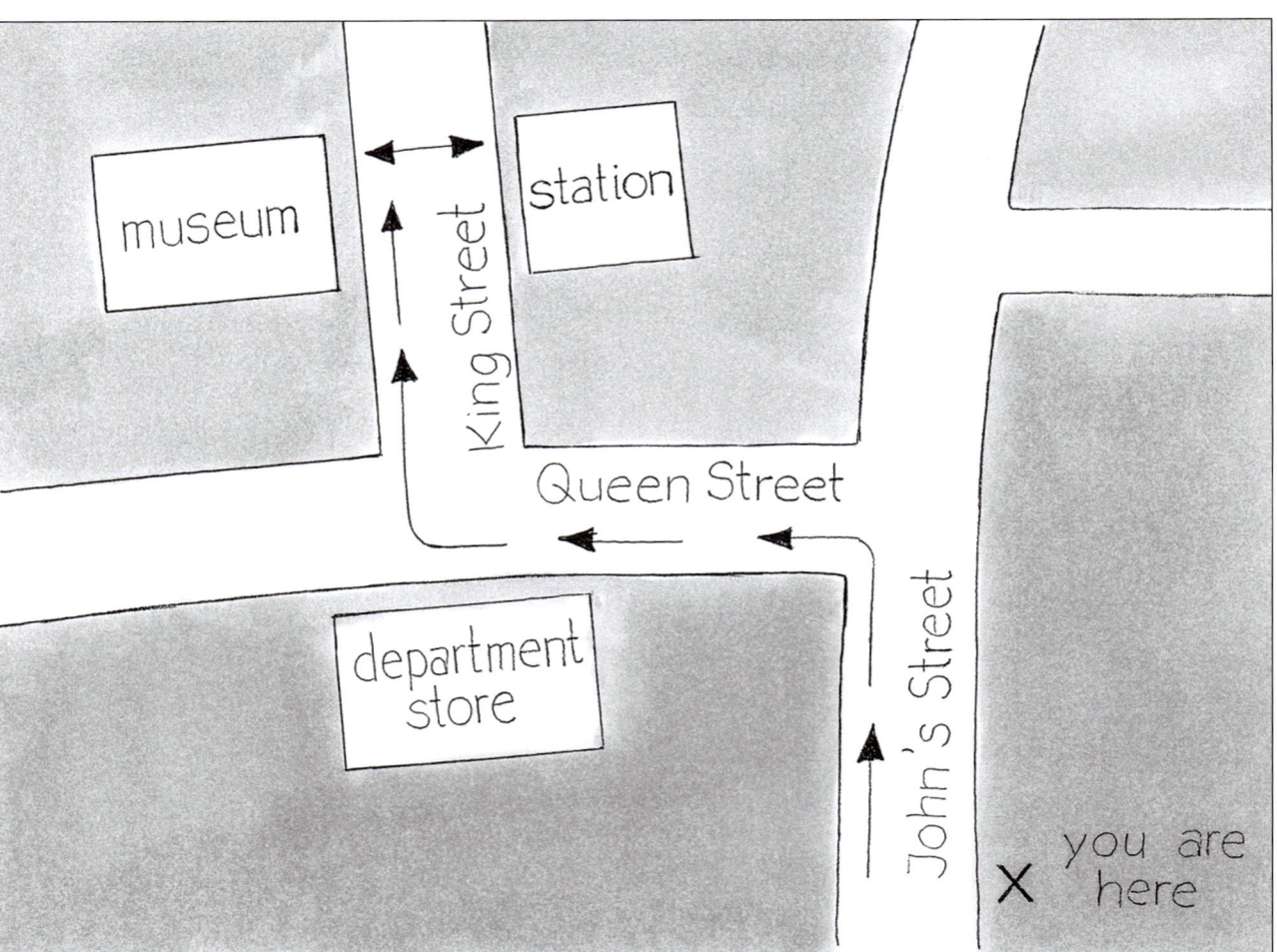

A tourist asks you the way from John's Street to the station. Write the dialogue:

Tourist Excuse me, _____.

You _____ John's Street. (1)

Then _____

_____

_____.

The station is _____.

Tourist _____.

Unit 6 | Klassenarbeit B

3 STUDY SKILLS Correcting mistakes: Sara's invitation   ____ / 5

Sara has written invitation cards for her birthday. Correct the five spelling mistakes.
Cross out (✗) the wrong words and write down the text again with the right words. Underline them.

> Dear Sue,
> It's my birthday soon, so I'd like to invit you to my party.
> It's a special party – a roman party.
> The party will be on
>
> 5th July from 2 pm to 8 pm.
>
> We'll meat at my house first and
> than cycle to the museum together.
>
> I hope you can come.
> Let me no soon if you can come.
>
> Love Sara

    Lies den Text langsam und aufmerksam, damit du die Rechtschreibfehler findest.
    Achte auf:
    – Vollständigkeit der Wörter: Sind alle Buchstaben da?
    – Auf Groß und Kleinschreibung: Was wird im Englischen großgeschrieben?
    – Ist es das richtige Wort? Z. B. *see = sehen* oder *sea = Meer*?

4 GRAMMAR When Sara's mum arrived   ___/4

Benny says what these people were doing when Sara's mum arrived at the Roman Baths birthday party.

When Sara's mum arrived …

Pete _____.

I _____.

Sara _____.

Sophie and Lucy _____.

> ☞ Das **Past progressive** wird mit was/were + ing-Form gebildet.
> Es wird oft benutzt, um auszudrücken, was gerade vor sich ging, als eine zweite Handlung einsetzte: Jemand war gerade dabei etwas zu tun, als …

Unit 6 | Klassenarbeit B

WRITING

___/ 17

Birthday party at the Roman Baths

Sue was one of Sara's guests. Look at the pictures and write a text for Sue's diary.
Say what you liked and what was funny. Use some of the linking words and adjectives in the box.

Linking words	Adjectives
at two o'clock • a few minutes • later • suddenly • then • next • so • but	funny • interesting • nice • great • amazing • beautiful • best • difficult • easy • exciting • fantastic • favourite • happy

1 meet – Sara's house

2 cycle to

3 man – tell plans for the afternoon

4 bring – Roman clothes
   put on – laugh

5 have – drinks, …

6 go round – look at

7 make sandals

8 cycle home

Dear diary,
Today I went to Sara's birthday party. We met …

> Wenn du im Tagebuch über **Vergangenes** berichtest, verwendest du das **Simple past**:
> I talk<u>ed</u> to my friend …
>
> Die volle Punktzahl bekommst du, wenn deine Lösung richtig ist und du die Arbeitsanweisung genau befolgt hast:
> • Überprüfe, ob du geschrieben hast, was dir gefallen hat und was du lustig fandest.
> • Überprüfe ob du **linking words** und **Adjektive** benutzt hast.

Kompetenztest

Im Laufe deines bisherigen Englischunterrichts hast du Hören, Lesen, Schreiben und Sprechen trainiert. Diese Kompetenzen benötigst du, um die englische Sprache zu beherrschen. Mithilfe dieses Kompetenztests kannst du einschätzen, welche dieser Fähigkeiten du schon kannst und welche du noch üben musst. An vielen Schulen werden in Klasse 6 Kompetenztests geschrieben. Sie werden auch Diagnosetests oder Vergleichsarbeiten genannt. Hier kannst du dich auf die Testsituation vorbereiten.
Du hast 60 Minuten Zeit.

Gesamtpunktzahl _____ / 80   Note _____

TEIL 1: LISTENING

_____ / 20

🎧 19 AT A PARK IN PARIS

There is an international skateboard contest in a park in Paris. Lily and Philip are watching.
They meet Charlie. Listen to Charlie, Lily and Philip.

1 Countries and places

_____ / 4

Listen for the names of these countries or cities and tick (✔) them if you hear them.
*You must tick **four** boxes.*

1	Chester	
2	Gloucester	
3	Berlin	
4	Paris	
5	Belgium	

6	Dover	
7	England	
8	Germany	
9	London	
10	France	

2 Charlie and Philip

_____ / 8

Listen again. What is correct about Charlie and Philip?
Decide if the sentence is right for Charlie or for Philip. You must tick (✔) eight boxes.

		Charlie	Philip
1	He is Lily's twin brother.		
2	He is from Dover.		
3	He is from Chester.		
4	His new school is great.		
5	He is on holiday in Paris.		
6	He lives in Paris.		
7	He came to Paris on Tuesday.		
8	He is with his uncle George.		

3 All about Lily and Philip's parents

_____ / 8

Listen again. Are these sentences right or wrong? Tick (✔) the right box.

		Right	Wrong
1	Their mum and dad are French.	☐	☐
2	Their parents live in a park.	☐	☐
3	Their mum likes Paris.	☐	☐
4	Their dad has a job in Paris.	☐	☐
5	Their dad worked in Dover.	☐	☐
6	Their dad didn't like his job in Chester.	☐	☐
7	Their dad loved English food.	☐	☐
8	Their dad likes Paris.	☐	☐

TEIL 2: SPEAKING

_____ / 20

1 At lunch break

_____ / 8

What can you see in this photo?

Where are these students?

What time of the day is it?

Why are they together?

What have they got on the table?

What are they doing?

2 Your first day at a new school

🎧 20

____ / 12

You and your family have moved to another city. Today is your first day at the new school.
Your English teacher asks you some questions.

Teacher Welcome to our school. Today is your first day, isn't it? It's good to have you here. How are you?

You ...

Teacher What's your name?

You ...

Teacher How old are you?

You ...

Teacher Where are you from?

You ...

Teacher Tell us something about your old school: the teachers, the students and your favourite subjects ...

You ...

Teacher Have you got brothers or sisters?

You ...

Teacher What do you do in your free time?

You ...

Teacher Tell us something about your last holiday: what was it like, where did you go and what did you do?

You ...

Teacher That sounds interesting. Well, I'm sure you'll like it here at our school. The students here are really nice. So, all the best. Have a great first day!

TEIL 3: READING

___ / 20

Gwen's holiday diary

Saturday

It was grey and cold when we started from Chester this morning. There was a lot of traffic, so it took us a long time to get to Kendal and we had to stop three times on the way because of Benny. He is nine, but he is a big baby. When we arrived in Kendal, it was too late for most things, so we went to *Kendal Leisure Centre*. It closes at eleven pm. Dad went to the sauna. Mum played with Benny in the baby pool. (Why can't he play with other kids?) I swam and I did the 50 metres in only a minute. Then we had fish and chips and ice cream. Benny didn't like his ice cream, so I had two.

Our bed & breakfast place is OK. The bad thing is that Benny and I have to be in one room together. I want to read my book but Benny says he can't sleep because of the lamp. Why can't he just shut his eyes?

Sunday

It was a wet Sunday. No sun. But it wasn't a problem. *Lakeland Climbing Centre* is not outside. It's the biggest rock-climbing centre in the north of England and home to 'Kendal Wall', a great wall to climb. I made it all the way up!

In the afternoon the sun was out. Mum wanted to see the *Topiary Gardens*. It was boring – only old trees, but we had tea there at the Tea Room. Benny had hot chocolate, but he didn't drink it all, so I had tea and hot chocolate.

1 On the way to Kendal

___ / 4

Tick (✔) the right ending. More than one ending can be correct for the numbers 1–3. You must tick 4 endings.

1	When they started it was	a) morning.	☐
		b) afternoon.	☐
		c) evening.	☐
		d) Saturday.	☐
		e) Sunday.	☐
		f) nice.	☐

2	On the way to Kendal	a) they went very fast.	☐
		b) they had tea.	☐
		c) there was an accident.	☐
		d) they needed lots of time.	☐

3	When they arrived in Kendal	a) it was eleven in the morning.	☐
		b) it was eleven in the evening.	☐
		c) it was late.	☐
		d) everybody had ice cream.	☐

2 In Kendal on Saturday ___/6

Tick (✔) the right box.

		Right	Wrong	Not in the text
1	They all went swimming at *Kendal Leisure Centre*.	☐	☐	☐
2	At *Kendal Leisure Centre* Gwen's mother bought Benny something to drink.	☐	☐	☐
3	Gwen's brother Benny is still a baby. He is nine months old.	☐	☐	☐
4	*Kendal Leisure Centre* is open late.	☐	☐	☐
5	Benny can't swim.	☐	☐	☐
6	Gwen is not happy because Benny and she have to sleep in the same room.	☐	☐	☐

3 In Kendal on Sunday ___/7

Tick (✔) the right box.

		Right	Wrong	Not in the text
1	Sunday morning was nice.	☐	☐	☐
2	*Lakeland Climbing Centre* has no roof.	☐	☐	☐
3	It's the biggest climbing centre in England.	☐	☐	☐
4	*Kendal Wall* is 20 metres high.	☐	☐	☐
5	The *Topiary Gardens* are near the *Kendal Wall*.	☐	☐	☐
6	You can have a tea at the *Topiary Gardens*.	☐	☐	☐
7	Gwen drank hot chocolate there.	☐	☐	☐

4 Gwen ___/3

Tick (✔) the right ending.

1	Gwen has got a brother. He's nine	a) and she likes playing with him.	☐
		b) and he doesn't like long trips in the car.	☐

2	On Saturday evening Gwen is angry because	a) Benny won't let her read.	☐
		b) Benny is talking to her.	☐

3	Gwen likes	a) climbing.	☐
		b) walking round parks and gardens.	☐

TEIL 4: WORDS AND WRITING

1 WORDS A trip to Wales

Complete the mind map.

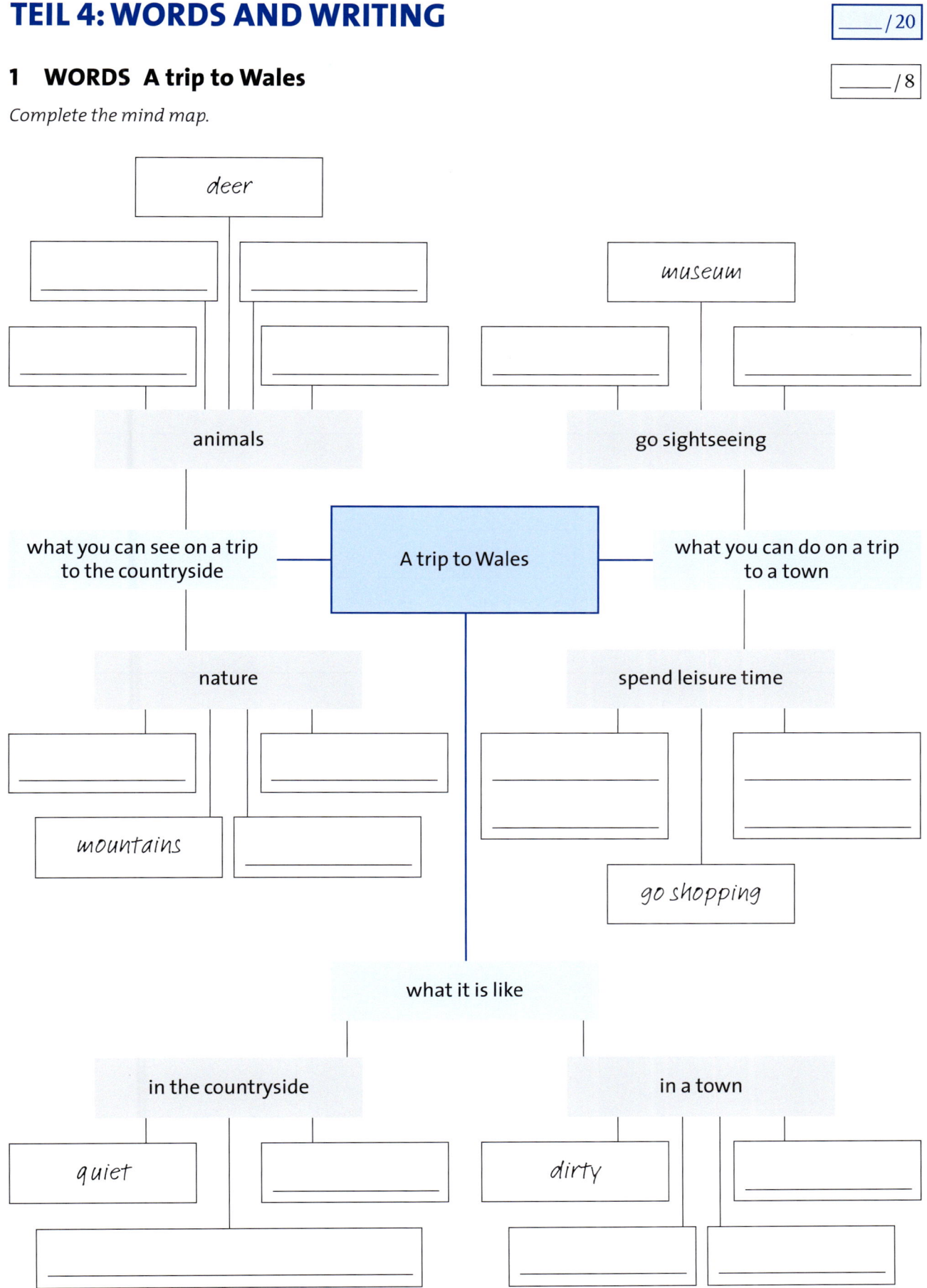

2 WRITING An e-mail about your last holiday

____ / 12

Write an e-mail to your penfriend Steve about your last holiday.

Write a beginning and an ending. Tell him: • when you went (1P) • where you went (1P) • who went with you (1P) • where you stayed (1P) • what you did (2P) • what you liked about it (2P) • what you didn't like about it (2P)	Use 'little' words from the list to make your sentences. • and • so • but • too • also

English G 21

Klassenarbeitstrainer
für Schülerinnen und Schüler

Lösungen und Lerntipps

D2

Cornelsen

Welcome back — Lösungen

LISTENING

🎧 01 Paul's very special holiday

Reporter	Hello everybody. You're listening to "Bristol Today", the radio programme for families. Today we are talking to Paul about a very special holiday. Hello, Paul. Tell us, what was special about your holiday?
Paul	Well, my family and I went on a 3 weeks' trip around the world. We were the winners in a TV show and the prize was this trip around the world.
Reporter	Wow! That sounds very interesting. Paul, where did you go?
Paul	Well, we started our trip in London. First we flew to France, then to Spain, Germany and Italy. We then went to the USA. Our next stop was in China, where we stayed for 4 days. Our last stop was in Sydney, Australia. And then we had to go home again.
Reporter	Now Paul, what were your favourite places?
Paul	Well, there were many of course. I liked Paris with all the museums. I can't speak a word of French. But we had warm and sunny weather and went to many cafés. In Berlin we went to the Brandenburg Gate and on a boat trip – but it was windy and a bit rainy. Oh, and I liked the German Museum in Munich. It rained and it was cold but we had a great time. I want to go there again.
Reporter	What about the other countries?
Paul	Oh, in Italy I liked the people – they were always so nice and I liked the spaghetti. In Rome the weather was super – you know, not too hot and not too cold, just warm. In New York I went shopping. We were lucky again – it was warm and sunny so it was great to go shopping. It was interesting to see all the shops. I have many souvenirs at home now. In Miami in Florida the weather was hot so we went to the beach a lot. We really had a great time there.
Reporter	So you relaxed in Florida, did you?
Paul	Yes, we did, before we flew to China for three days. We stopped in Beijing where we needed our rain jackets a lot. Then we went to Shanghai to see my Uncle Mike. Our last stop was in Sydney, Australia. It wasn't too hot there because it was wintertime. But it was warm enough to go surfing. One day it was stormy. The three weeks were over so quickly. And here I am back home again.
Reporter	Thanks a lot for the interview, Paul. Bye.

1 Where did Paul go?

Germany, Italy, France, Spain, USA, China, Australia

2 What was the weather like?

	warm	cold	sunny	rainy	hot	windy	stormy
Paris	✔		✔				
Berlin				✔		✔	
Munich (München)		✔		✔			
Rome (Rom)	✔						
New York	✔		✔				
Miami					✔		
Beijing (Peking)				✔			
Sydney	✔						✔

TEIL 4: WORDS AND WRITING

1 WORDS A trip to Wales

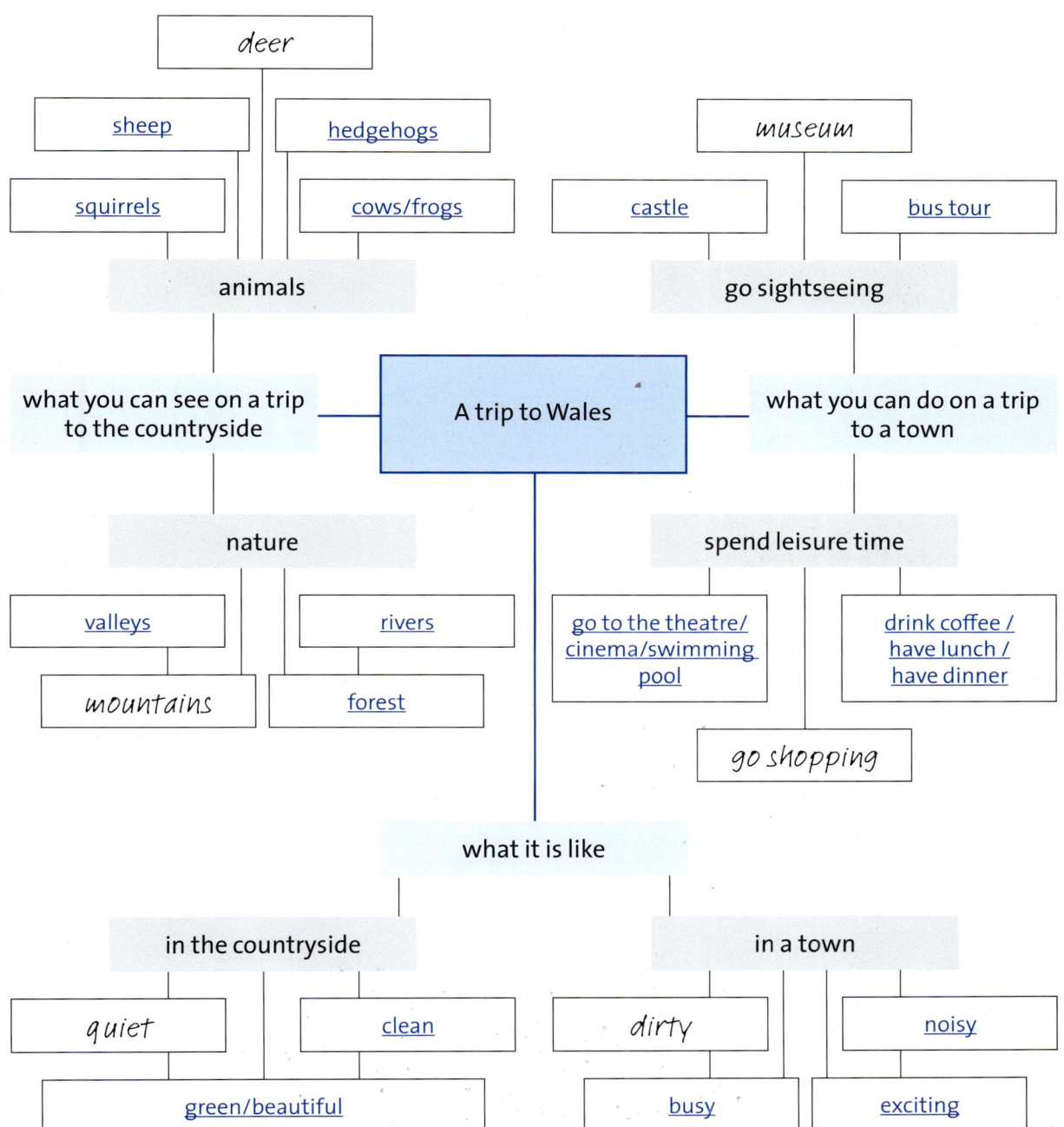

2 WRITING An e-mail about your last holiday

Mögliche Lösung:

Hi Steve, (0,5P)

Last month I went on holiday to Italy. (2P) I went there with my parents and my brother. (1P) We stayed in a caravan near the beach, so we could go swimming every day. (2P) On some days we went on trips to visit a town. (1P) I liked the weather and the fantastic ice cream – I had one every day. (2P) My brother always wanted to read and never played with me. (1P) That was very boring. (1P) I missed my friends too. (1P)

See you, … (0,5P)

TEIL 3: READING

Gwen's holiday diary

1 On the way to Kendal

1a, d   2d   3c

2 In Kendal on Saturday

		Right	Wrong	Not in the text
1	They all went swimming at *Kendal Leisure Centre*.		✔	
2	At *Kendal Leisure Centre* Gwen's mother bought Benny something to drink.			✔
3	Gwen's brother Benny is still a baby. He is nine months old.		✔	
4	*Kendal Leisure Centre* is open late.	✔		
5	Benny can't swim.			✔
6	Gwen is not happy because Benny and she have to sleep in the same room.	✔		

3 In Kendal on Sunday

		Right	Wrong	Not in the text
1	Sunday morning was nice.		✔	
2	*Lakeland Climbing Centre* has no roof.		✔	
3	It's the biggest climbing centre in England.		✔	
4	*Kendal Wall* is 20 metres high.			✔
5	The *Topiary Gardens* are near the Kendal Wall.			✔
6	You can have a tea at the *Topiary Gardens*.	✔		
7	Gwen drank hot chocolate there.	✔		

4 Gwen

1b   2a   3a

TEIL 2: SPEAKING

1 At lunch break

Mögliche Lösung:

In the picture I can see some students at school. (1P) It's probably 1 o'clock / 2 o'clock in the afternoon. (1P) They are together because they want to have lunch. (2P) On the table they have, bananas, apples, apple juice, orange juice and plates with burgers. (2P) They are having lunch and they are talking. (1P) The girl on the left is laughing. (1P)

🎧 20 2 Your first day at a new school

Mögliche Lösung:

Teacher	Welcome to our school. Today is your first day, isn't it? It's good to have you here. How are you?	
You	I'm fine, thanks.	(0,5P)
Teacher	What's your name?	
You	My name is …	(0,5P)
Teacher	How old are you?	
You	I'm … years old.	(0,5P)
Teacher	Where are you from?	
You	I'm from …	(0,5P)
Teacher	Tell us something about your old school: the teachers, the students and your favourite subjects …	
You	My form teacher was very nice. And most students were OK. I had a lot of friends there. My favourite subjects were/are …	(3P)
Teacher	Have you got brothers or sisters?	
You	Yes, I have. I've got a younger brother, he's eight, and an older sister, she is ten.	(2P)
Teacher	What do you do in your free time?	
You	I listen to music and I play football.	(2P)
Teacher	Tell us something about your last holiday: what was it like, where did you go and what did you do?	
You	It was fantastic. We went to … We went to the beach every day. / We went on bike rides. / We visited museums. / …	(3P)
Teacher	That sounds interesting. Well, I'm sure you'll like it here at our school. The students here are really nice. So, all the best. Have a great first day!	

2 Charlie and Philip

	Charlie	Philip
1 He is Lily's twin brother.		✔
2 He is from Dover.		✔
3 He is from Chester.	✔	
4 His new school is great.		✔
5 He is on holiday in Paris.	✔	
6 He lives in Paris.		✔
7 He came to Paris on Tuesday.	✔	
8 He is with his uncle George.	✔	

3 All about Lily and Philip's parents

	Right	Wrong
1 Their mum and dad are French.		✔
2 Their parents live in a park.		✔
3 Their mum likes Paris.		✔
4 Their dad has a job in Paris.	✔	
5 Their dad worked in Dover.	✔	
6 Their dad didn't like his job in Chester.		✔
7 Their dad loved English food.		✔
8 Their dad likes Paris.	✔	

TEIL 1: LISTENING

🎧 19 **At a park in Paris**

Charlie	Hi, I'm Charlie. What's your name?
Lily	I'm Lily and this is my twin brother Philip.
Charlie	Hi, Philip. Where are you from?
Philip	We're from Dover, but now we live in Paris.
Charlie	But you're English, aren't you?
Lily	Well, Mum's English but Dad's French. First we lived in England and now we live here in Paris.
Philip	We live behind this park.
Charlie	Do you speak French?
Lily	We don't speak French at home, but we *must* speak French at school now. I don't like it.
Philip	I like it here. Paris is great. Our new school is great and my new friends are great, too.
Lily	Paris is great for you, Philip, but it isn't for me and it isn't for Mum.
Charlie	Why didn't you stay in England?
Lily	Because Dad started a new job here in Paris. He worked in Dover but he didn't like it. It wasn't the right job for him and it wasn't the right place. He never liked the English weather or our English food. But here he is very happy.
Philip	And I'm happy too.
Lily	Yes, Philip, we know. Paris is fantastic and Dover is boring.
Philip	Where are you from, Charlie?
Charlie	I'm from Chester. We are on holiday. I came here on Tuesday with my parents and my Uncle George.
Philip	That's only three days ago. Did you come by car?
Charlie	No, not by car, by train. Dad doesn't like the traffic in Paris.
Lily	Yeah, traffic is *really* bad here.
Philip	You don't need a car in Paris. There's the Metro. You can take the underground trains to all the places.
Lily	It doesn't go to all places. The Metro doesn't go to England.
Philip	Oh Lily, why don't you go back to England with Charlie?
Lily	Just be quiet now, Philip and let's watch the contest!

1 Countries and places

1	Chester	✔
2	Gloucester	
3	Berlin	
4	Paris	✔
5	Belgium	

6	Dover	✔
7	England	✔
8	Germany	
9	London	
10	France	

4 GRAMMAR When Sara's mum arrived

When Sara's mum arrived ...

Pete <u>was making sandals</u>.

I <u>was looking at old Roman plates</u>.

Sara <u>was learning some Latin words</u>.

Sophie and Lucy <u>were eating sandwiches</u>.

WRITING

Birthday party at the Roman Baths

Today I went to Sara's birthday party. We met at Sarah's house at 2 pm. (1P) Then we all cycled to the Roman Baths. (1P) In the museum a young man / Matthew told us the plans for the afternoon. (1P) Then he brought the Roman clothes for us. (1P) We put them on – that was really funny and we laughed. (2P) We had some drinks, biscuits and sandwiches. (2P) After that we went round the museum and looked at all the Roman things. (2P) I thought that was very interesting. (1P) Then we made our own Roman sandals. (1P) It was super. I like my sandals very much. (2P) At 7 pm we cycled back to Sara's house. (1P) It was a great day!! (1P)

3 STUDY SKILLS Correcting mistakes: Sara's invitation

Dear Sue,

it's my birthday soon, so I'd like to <u>invite</u> you to my party. It's a special party – a <u>Roman</u> party.

The party will be on **5th July from 2 pm to 8 pm**.

We'll <u>meet</u> at my house first and <u>then</u> cycle to the museum together. I hope you can come.

Let me <u>know</u> soon if you can come.

Love Sara

Lerntipp So kannst du **Fehler vermeiden**:

■ Mache dir klar, welches Rechtschreibproblem hinter einem Fehlerwort steckt. Wähle dazu aus der unten angegebenen Liste aus und trage dann die Nummer des Rechschreibproblems zum jeweiligen Fehlerwort:

Fehlerwort ▶	Korrektur	Nummer des Problems
~~invit~~	invite	
~~roman~~	Roman	
~~meat~~	meet	
~~than~~	then	
~~no~~	know	

Liste von Rechtschreibproblemen:

1 groß oder klein?

Im Englischen wird großgeschrieben:
– am Satzanfang
– I (= ich)
– Eigennamen (Länder-, Wochentags-, Monatsnamen, Feiertage)
– das zu einem Land / einer Region gehörende Adjektiv (Roman, German, …)
– Bezeichnung für Menschen aus unterschiedlichen Ländern / Regionen
   (the Americans, the French, the Romans, …)

2 Bedeutung des Wortes:

Bei manchen Wörtern ändert sich die Bedeutung je nach Schreibung:

meat = Fleisch	meet = treffen
no = nein	know = wissen
week = Woche	weak = schwach
see = sehen	sea = Meer

3 Vollständigkeit eines Wortes:

Sind alle Buchstaben vorhanden?

■ Führe ein kleines Heft mit deinen persönlichen Fehlerwörtern. Immer wenn du ein Wort nicht richtig geschrieben hast, notierst du das Fehlerwort und die Korrektur. Schreibe dahinter, um welches Rechtschreibproblem es sich handelt.
Bevor du einen Text schreibst oder vor Klassenarbeiten, wiederholst du diese Fehlerwörter noch einmal, indem du sie z. B dreimal schreibst.

Unit 6 | Lösungen B

LANGUAGE

1 WORDS Word building

a)

Zusammensetzungen, bei denen die Wörter getrennt bleiben	Zusammensetzungen, bei denen die Wörter zusammengeschrieben werden
post office, police station, department store, leisure centre, pocket money	caretaker, grandfather, sweetheart, headache, woodpecker

b)

everybody, weekend, building, information, player, department

> **Lerntipp** So kannst du **Word building** üben
>
> Schreibe die Wortteile aus der Aufgabe auf kleine Zettel und lege sie aneinander. So ist es einfacher, die passenden Wortteile zu finden.

2 WORDS Can you tell me the way?

Tourist Excuse me, how do I get to the station? / can you tell me the way to the station, please? (1P)

You Go along John's Street. (1)

 Then turn left into Queen Street. (1)

 Go straight on. (1)

 At the department store on the left, turn right into King Street. (1)

 The station is opposite the museum. (1)

Tourist Thank you very much. (1P)

Lösungen B

LISTENING

🎧 18 **A birthday party at the Roman Baths**

Matthew   Hello everybody. How are you today? Welcome to our birthday party for Sara.
Hello, Sara and happy birthday to you. It's great to have you here. I'm Matthew and I've prepared the party for you. Let me explain what we are going to do this afternoon: Well, we are going on a trip to Roman times.

In a minute I will get out the Roman costumes for you, so that you can feel like real Romans. Then of course we will have some drinks, some biscuits and sandwiches. They're not Roman, but I hope you will like them. We will then go round the Roman Baths and find out more about the Roman life.

Then you can choose one of three activities: you can make your own Roman sandals, or you can try to find old things in the sand, or you can learn some Latin words and a Latin birthday poem.

I'll go and get the costumes and you can talk about what you would like to do.

Benny   It's Sara's birthday, so I think she must say what she likes best.

Sara   Thank you, Benny. Well, it's difficult, really. I would like to do all three things. But I think making the sandals will be a good idea. And – I would like to learn some Latin words.

Benny   I know what – we'll ask him if we can learn "Happy birthday" in Latin, OK everybody?

Matthew   So, here are your costumes …

…

Sara   Well, I liked the tour.

Benny   Yes, so did I.

Matthew   What would you like to do now?

Sara   Can we make sandals and learn Happy Birthday in Latin, please?

Matthew   I'm sorry there's not enough time to do two things. Making sandals is good fun. And you can take them home with you as a souvenir. So what do you think?

Sara   Let's make the sandals then.

1 Sara's Roman birthday

Numbers of the pictures: 1, 3, 5

2 All about the party

		Right	Wrong
1	They will go swimming.		✔
2	They will get something to eat and to drink at the Roman Baths.	✔	
3	Sara and her friends will find out more about how the Romans lived.	✔	
4	They can choose one activity.	✔	
5	It's easy for Sara to choose the most interesting activity.		✔
6	Sara's friends want to look for things in the sand.		✔
7	Matthew teaches them some Latin words.		✔
8	At the end of the party every child has got a pair of Roman sandals.	✔	

SPEAKING

🎧 16 **Learn English in Bath!**

🎧 17 **Now you**

Mögliche Lösung:

Reporter	Hello. Let's start with some information about yourself: what's your name, where are you from and how old are you?
Julian	Hi. I'm Julian and I'm from Leipzig, Germany. I'm 16 years old. (1)
Reporter	Well, tell us why you came to Bath.
Julian	I came here because my English isn't very good. I can write well but I find it difficult to speak English. (3)
Reporter	I understand. Now, do you like it here at the school?
Julian	Yes, I do. I think the school is OK. (1)
Reporter	What do you like best?
Julian	I like the other students. They come from different countries. I've met some nice friends. / I am really happy with my host family. Their son is very nice. He is 16 and we can do things together. (3)
Reporter	What do you think: has your English become better?
Julian	Yes, it has. It's easier for me to speak English now. I talk a lot to my friends at the language school. (2)
Reporter	What about Bath? Do you like it?
Julian	Yes, I do. I think Bath is a nice town. I like the discos. (2)
Reporter	What have you already visited here in Bath?
Julian	I have visited the Roman Baths and the Herschel Museum / the Museum of Costume / … That was really interesting. (2)
Reporter	Thank you.
Julian	You're welcome. (1P)

> **Lerntipp** So kannst du üben, dich **freundlich auf Englisch zu unterhalten**.
>
> ▪ Lies das **Skills File Talking to people** in deinem Englischbuch auf S. 128 durch.
> ▪ Halte dann das Gespräch in b) zwischen Malte und Debbie und verändere das Gespräch zwischen Jenny und Jan in a) so, dass Jan freundlicher klingt.
> ▪ Wiederhole dann die Übung im Klassenarbeitstrainer und achte auf freundliche Antworten. Höre dir dazu das Interview mit José noch einmal an und notiere dir Teile, die du übernehmen kannst.

MEDIATION

Get to know Bath – Come and enjoy our bus tours

Vater Diese Tour sieht sehr interessant aus. Wie lange dauert sie?

Du Sie dauert eine Stunde. (1)

Vater Ist das so eine Besichtigungstour, auf der man alles von einem Tonband erklärt bekommt? Das finde ich nämlich nicht so gut.

Du Nein, es gibt einen Fremdenführer, der alles erklärt und auf alle Fragen antwortet. (2)

Vater Das ist gut. Steht da, was man alles besichtigen kann?

Du Also, natürlich die römischen Bäder, außerdem das älteste Haus in Bath, das Kostümmuseum, das William Herschel Haus, den Royal Victoria Park und den „Circus". (2)

Vater Kann man denn auch in den Zirkus gehen oder was soll das bedeuten?

Du Der „Circus" ist eine runde Straße in Bath. (1)

Vater Die englischen Parks gefallen mir gut. Kann man sich da auch aufhalten oder muss man immer bei der Gruppe bleiben?

Du Man kann aussteigen, etwas besichtigen und später wieder in den nächsten Bus einsteigen. (2)

Vater Jetzt noch zu den Preisen: Wir sind ja 2 Erwachsene und zwei Kinder. Sara ist 6 und Peter, du bist 13. Was ist da am preiswertesten?

Du Es gibt 2 Angebote: das Familienticket für 15 Pfund oder das Familienticket für 30 Pfund, das schließt den Eintritt / die Eintrittskarte für die Roman Baths mit ein. (3)

Vater Dann nehmen wir das mit dem Eintritt für die Roman Baths, denn die wollen wir ja unbedingt besichtigen. Wo können wir die Tickets kaufen?

Du Wir können Sie übers Internet kaufen oder in der Touristeninformation in Bath. (1P)

Lerntipp	So kannst du **Präpositionen** lernen

- Lerne bei neuen Wörtern die zugehörige Präposition immer gleich mit, z. B. **at** 5 o'clock, wait **for**.
- Achte besonders auf Verben mit verschiedenen Präpositionen: z.B. *look **at** , look **for**, look **after** ...* Hier ändert sich je nach Präposition die Bedeutung: *look at* = anschauen, *look for* = suchen, *look after* = sich kümmern um.
- Lege dir in deinem Lernheft eine Liste an mit Verben + Präposition. Notiere dir jeweils auch die deutsche Bedeutung.
- Wähle aus deiner Liste fünf Verben mit Präposition aus und bilde Sätze.

4 GRAMMAR What are they doing?

1 Mr and Mrs Smith are sitting in a café.
2 A girl is asking the way to Oxford Road.
3 Susan and her mother are going shopping.
4 Mrs Günter and her daughters are visiting the Roman Baths.
5 José is learning English.
6 A woman is waiting for the bus.

Lerntipp	Das **Present-progressive**-Fahrrad

Fall nicht vom Rad!
Das **present progressive** hat <u>immer</u>
ein Vorderrad ▶ **am, are, is; am / 'm** not; **isn't; aren't**
ein Pedal ▶ **Verb**
ein Hinterrad ▶ **-ing**.

Wenn du auf das Pedal = **Verb** trittst, dann ist die Handlung im Gang ▶ **present progressive**.

So kannst du üben, das **present progressive** richtig zu bilden:
Sammle aus deinem Buch oder deinem Workbook Sätze mit dem **present progressive**.
Zeichne das **Present-progressive**-Fahrrad ein. ▶ Mache einen Kreis (Vorderrad) um **am, are, is** und einen Kreis (Hinterrad) um **-ing**.

Ergänze das 'Vorderrad'.

			Zum Überprüfen:
Singular	1. Person	I ◯ not listen**ing** to the radio.	I **am** not listening to the radio.
	2. Person	◯ you listen**ing** to the radio?	**Are** you listening to the radio?
	3. Person	Jessica ◯ tidy**ing** the living room.	Jessica **is** tidying the living room.
		◯ Luke help**ing** her?	**Is** Luke helping her?
Plural	1. Person	We ◯ danc**ing** to the music.	We **are** dancing to the music.
	2. Person	◯ you watch**ing** us?	**Are** you watching us?
	3. Person	They ◯ eat**ing** chips.	They **are** eating chips.
Überprüfe anhand der dritten Spalte, ob du alles richtig hast.			

Unit 6 | Lösungen A

LANGUAGE

1 WORDS In the city

a)

post office, police station, restaurant, chemist, school, department store, leisure centre, museum, station, shop, cinema, café, castle, tourist information centre, church, …   (5P)

b)

1 Go straight on.
2 Turn right.
3 Turn left.
4 Cross the road.
5 Go past the curch.

> **Lerntipp** So kannst du **Wörter wiederholen**. Wähle aus:
>
> ■ Bereite ein liniertes DIN-A4-Blatt vor, indem du jeden Buchstaben des Alphabets jeweils an den Anfang einer Linie schreibst. Nimm dir dann ein Wortfeld (z. B. *In the city*) vor und schreibe zu jedem Buchstaben möglichst mehrere Wörter. Notiere Substantive, Verben und Adjektive.
>
> ■ Sammle die verschiedenen Wörter in einer Mindmap. Nimm ein Wortfeld (z. B. *In the city*), schreibe es in die Mitte und finde weitere Oberbegriffe, zu denen du dann Wörter ergänzen kannst. Beispiele für Oberbegriffe sind: *where you can go, what you can do, telling the way, …*

2 WORDS Find the words.

1 One hundred years are a century.
2 If you have a room with a window you can see out.
3 When you are very tired, you must often yawn.
4 You can go there to have lunch or dinner: restaurant.
5 In Britain the school year has three terms.
6 At the end of a play, people sometimes cheer loudly.
7 If you put the letters in the boxes in the right order you get a word for the people who watch a play: audience.

3 WORDS About the tourists in Bath

1 Susan and her mother are sitting at a table in a café.
2 They will cycle back to Bristol.
3 José wants to have a look at the Roman Baths too.
4 At 5 o'clock he wants to visit the Roman Baths with his friends.
5 Many visitors want to see the old costumes at the Museum of Costumes.
6 On Wednesdays it is open until 10 pm.

Lösungen A

Unit 6

READING

Visitors in Bath

	Philip Smith	**Helen Günter**	**Susan**	**José**
where from?	from Gloucester	from Germany/ Heitersheim	from Bristol	from Spain/Madrid
in Bath alone / together with?	with his wife	with her two daughters	with her mum	alone / with 19 other students
how long in Bath?	1 day	2 days	1 day	3 weeks
in Bath for the first time?	yes	no	no	yes
activities in the past this week	Wales	flew to London and went to Bath by train	Roman Baths, William Herschel Museum	went to London
activities today	Roman Baths	Roman Baths	shopping	Roman Baths
activities in the next days	Museum of Costume	Scotland	visit the Museum of Costume	visit Bristol

> **Lerntipp**   Scanning – So kannst du Texte gezielt nach Informationen absuchen:
> - Lies das **Skills File Scanning** in deinem Englischbuch auf S. 126 durch.
> - Wende dann die Methode des Scanning auf den Text „Moles" auf derselben Seite an.
> - Übe Scanning mit Aufgabe 8 auf der S. 47 und Aufgabe 12a auf S. 52 in deinem Englischbuch

SPEAKING

🎧 15 **Let's present our new game**

Now you

Mögliche Notizen:

You must talk about:	Your ideas:
name of the game (1P)	"At the Zoo"
who was on your team? (1)	Peter, Mary, Neil and Nancy
how many players? how old? (1)	for four players, 12 to 101
what you need for the game (1)	a dice, the board, question cards, animals (counters)
idea of the game (2)	you must go round the zoo and visit as many animals as you can
what is special (red space, green space, questions, …)? (2)	red space: answer a question about animals blue space: miss a turn
who is the winner? (2)	you are the winner when you have visited all the animals

Mögliche Lösungen:

Hello everybody. We would like to present our game "At the Zoo". On our team were Peter, Mary, Neil and Nancy. Here you can see our box and the board.

The "At the Zoo" game is for four players from 12 to 101. You need a dice, the board, question cards, animals and counters.

You must go round the zoo and visit as many animals as you can. When you get to / land on a red space you must answer a question about animals. When you get to a blue space you miss a turn. When you have visited all the animals you are the winner.

Lerntipp So kannst du **Speaking Skills** üben:

- Höre dir die Präsentation mehrmals an.
- Schreibe dir besonders schwierige Sätze heraus und verwende sie in ähnlicher Form für deine eigene Präsentation.
- Schreibe dir deine gesamte Präsentation zunächst auf.
  Für deinen freien Vortrag solltest du dann aber nur Stichwörter verwenden.
- Tipps findest du auch auf S. 124 im **Skills File Giving a presentation** in deinem Englischbuch.

5 GRAMMAR How they worked

John read the instructions of the game quickly (quick).

The teams worked on their games very hard (hard).

Tim and Sandra talked about the game quietly (quiet).

The team presented their game proudly (proud).

Now you

Mögliche Lösungen:

Today I wrote nicely into my exercise book.

Today I went to school quickly.

> **Lerntipp** So kannst du die **Adverbien** üben:
> - Lies noch einmal im Grammar File auf S. 139 in deinem Englischbuch nach.
> - Schreibe die Besonderheiten in der Rechtschreibung und die unregelmäßigen Formen in dein Lernheft.

MEDIATION

A new game: The terrible red dragon

1. Es können 3–5 Spieler im Alter von 10–99 mitspielen. (1P)
2. Man benötigt ein Spielmännchen für jeden Spieler, einen Würfel, zwölf Kisten Gold, den Drachen und das Spielbrett. (3P)
3. Die Idee des Spieles: In einem Schloss haust ein hungriger Drachen, der die Spieler auffressen will. Die Spieler sind im Schloss, weil sie auf der Suche nach dem Gold sind. Aber der Weg durch das Schloss ist lang und gefährlich. (3P)
4. Beginn des Spieles: Man muss die Spielmännchen und den Drachen aufstellen. Der jüngste Spieler würfelt zuerst. Wenn er eine 4 würfelt, darf er anfangen. (2P)
5. Die Bedeutung der Felder:
   – Wenn man auf ein braunes Feld kommt, muss man einmal aussetzen.
   – Wenn man auf ein goldenes Feld kommt, darf man noch einmal würfeln und man bekommt eine Kiste Gold.
   – Wenn man auf ein schwarzes Feld kommt, rückt der Drache ein Feld näher.
   – Wenn man auf ein rotes Feld kommt, muss man dem Drachen eine Kiste Gold bezahlen. (4P)
6. Rolle des Drachens: Wenn der Drachen auf das Feld eines Spielmännchens kommt, frisst er dieses auf. (2P)
7. Man hat das Spiel gewonnen, wenn man als erste(r) oben im Schloss angekommen ist und die meisten Kisten Gold gesammelt hat. (2P)

2 GRAMMAR Plans for the game

1 Are you going to make a game about animals?
2 Is Peter going to work on the instructions?
3 Are you going to help John with the counters?
4 Aren't you going to make a box for your game?
5 When are you going to present your game to the class?

3 WORDS The Great Harbour Game

Sue I need some help. Can anybody help me please?

Mike OK. How can I help?

Sue Well, I'm drawing the board. I haven't got any good ideas for the pictures.

Mike What about pirates?

Sue That's a good idea.

Liz I can't find our ideas for the instructions. They must be somewhere.

Sue I've already looked for them and I couldn't see them anywhere.

Mike Oh, come on girls, somebody must have them.

Phil Here they are. Jill and I have added something.

Lerntipp So kannst du den Einsatz von **some** und **any** und deren Zusammensetzungen üben:

übertrage folgende Tabelle in dein Lernheft und suche entsprechende Sätze auf S. 169 in deinem Englischbuch.

+	−	?
There is somebody at the door.	I can't see anybody.	Can you see anybody in the garden?

4 GRAMMAR Are the games ready?

1 Sue hasn't painted the board.
2 Phil hasn't written the instructions.
3 Mike and Jill have made the six counters.
4 Liz has painted the box and written the name on it.

Lösungen B

Unit 5

READING

New games for everybody

1 Headings

1 c; 2 e; 3 d; 4 a; 5 b

2 About the week of the games

	Right	Wrong	Not in the text
1 The students of 6PF invented a new game together.		✔	
2 Every team got a topic from Mr Fisher.		✔	
3 Everybody in the team had a job.	✔		
4 At the beginning some teams had problems.			✔
5 They also made coloured boxes.	✔		
6 The instructions of the games weren't clear.			✔
7 The students of the best game got a present.			✔

> **Lerntipp** So kannst du **Reading skills** üben:
> - Nimm einen Markierstift zur Hand. Markiere die Stellen im Text, in denen du die Informationen für die Aufgaben findest.
> - Lies noch einmal das Skills File **Marking up a text** auf S. 127 in deinem Englischbuch.
> - Bearbeite Aufgabe 8 auf S. 83 in deinem Englischbuch.

LANGUAGE

1 WORDS Find the words

1 Smoothies are good and <u>healthy</u>.
2 You need this to play a board game: <u>dice</u>.
3 There are three sizes: small, medium and <u>large</u>.
4 You are buying something in a shop – you are a <u>customer</u>.
5 He brings your coffee in a café: <u>waiter</u>.
6 The smoothie is super. It's <u>delicious</u>.
7 The opposite of leave is <u>arrive</u>.
8 You open the door with a <u>key</u>.

Now you

<u>Teamwork</u> is when <u>some people work together on a job/task. They all want to finish this job well.</u>

Unit 5 | Lösungen A

3 GRAMMAR What are they going to do?

1 Team 1 isn't going to ask the head teacher.
2 It's going to work out the price for one smoothie.
3 Team 2 is going to ask the head teacher.
4 Team 3 isn't going to make good smoothies.
5 It's going to make the posters.
6 Team 2 and team 3 aren't going to put up the posters.
7 They are going to make good smoothies.
8 Team 1 and team 2 are going to put up the posters.

Now you

Mögliche Lösungen:

1 This afternoon I'm going to learn for the Maths test.
2 Next Saturday I'm going to think of a new game.
3 This afternoon I'm going to make smoothies.

4 STUDY SKILLS New attraction: Healthy but good

Zu markierende Textpassagen:

1 "… healthy and delicious smoothies …"
2 "… and sells them at a cheap price."
3 "… at lunch break."
4 "The head teacher thinks that the idea shows good teamwork."

Antworten:

1 The smoothies are healthy and delicious.
2 No, they are very cheap.
3 They sell them at lunch break.
4 Yes, she does.

WRITING

An e-mail to the Shocking Smoothies Team

Dear Shocking Smoothies team, (0,5)

I've read your article on the internet and like your idea very much. (2P) Maybe we want to open a smoothies bar at our school too. (2P) So I have many questions. (1P) How did you start? (1P) How many students are you? (1P) How much is one smoothie? / What about the price? (1P) Did you have any problems? (1P) Did you ask the head teacher before you started? (2P) What about the glasses? / Do you use glasses? (1P) Could you send me the recipe, please? (1P) Please write back soon. (1P)

Yours … (0,5P)

> **Lerntipp** So kannst du die **Fragebildung** im Englischen wiederholen:
>
> Schau im Lösungseinleger auf S. 11 nach. Dort findest du einen Kasten zur Fragebildung. Schreibe ihn erneut ab und fülle ihn mit neuen Beispielen.

2 More about the smoothies bar

		Right	Wrong
1	Alex liked the strawberry smoothie in the bar.	✔	
2	They want to go to the bar again tomorrow afternoon.		✔
3	Kerry thinks that smoothies at school are too difficult.	✔	
4	They don't need to ask the head teacher.		✔
5	They want to give all the money to Animal Helpline.		✔
6	They already know the price for one smoothie.		✔
7	The Smoothies team must clean the dirty glasses.		✔
8	They want to hang up posters.	✔	
9	They can't find a name for their bar.		✔

LANGUAGE

1 GETTING BY IN ENGLISH Say it in English

1 You're going the wrong way.
2 You're joking, aren't you.
3 Move back one space.
4 Whose turn is it?
5 Wait a minute.
6 Can you look after my dog?
7 This song is pretty cool.
8 Does anybody know whose purse this is?

2 WORDS Plurals of nouns

1 one dice — two dice
2 one strawberry — two strawberries
3 one waitress — two waitresses
4 one thief — two thieves
5 one wife — two wives
6 one man — two men
7 one woman — two women
8 one child — two children
9 one deer — two deer
10 one sheep — two sheep

Lerntipp So kannst du dir die **unregelmäßigen Pluralformen** merken:

- Sobald du ein Nomen mit einer unregelmäßigen Pluralform lernst, schreibst du es auf eine Karteikarte. Vorne schreibst du den Singular auf und hinten den Plural und die deutsche Übersetzung.
- Schreibe alle unregelmäßigen Pluralformen in eine Liste in dein Lernheft und ergänze sie regelmäßig:

Singular und Plural mit derselben Form	Sonderform im Plural
one sheep – two sheep	one child – two children

Unit 5 — Lösungen A

LISTENING

🎧 14 A great team: the "Shocking Smoothies"

Julie Hey Alex. I'm still thinking of that healthy juice bar.

Alex Yes, I think it's great. Do you remember the strawberry smoothie? It was delicious, wasn't it?

Julie Yes, you're right, Alex. And I could tell that you liked the strawberry smoothie – you had three of them, didn't you? Well, we could go there again this afternoon.

Alex This afternoon is fine. Wait a moment. Why don't we try and make smoothies at school? You know, for the other students. We could sell them at lunch break.

Ralph You mean, smoothies here at school? You're joking, aren't you, Alex?

Kerry I agree. We can't have smoothies at school. It's too difficult. Just think of all the glasses that we will need.

Alex Oh, come on, why not? Yes, there are some problems, but we can solve them. I'm sure. Then we can use the money for our next school trip and give some of it to Animal Helpline in Bristol. Oh come on!
Let's make a plan. First we must ask the head teacher. If she agrees, we can start.
Then we must try different smoothies so that we can make the best smoothies.
I think it will be best if we just use milk and fruit. What flavours would you like, Kerry?

Kerry I'd like strawberry, orange, banana and lemon.

Ralph What about the price? How much is one of our smoothies?

Alex Well Ralph, we must find out the prices for the milk and the fruit first. Then we can discuss the price.

Julie And what about the glasses? Where do we get all the glasses from? And who cleans them? The school will be full of dirty glasses.

Alex That's a big problem, really. Has anybody got an idea? You, Ralph?

Ralph Yes, – what about this? Everybody can bring a plastic glass, so that it's not dangerous.

Julie Great, this means we needn't clean the glasses. Super.

Alex So, now we can show that we are a good team. Who is going to do what?

Julie Kerry and I will try to make the different smoothies.

Ralph I'll go and ask the head teacher.

Alex Ralph and I find out about the prices. Have we forgotten anything? Yes, somebody must write posters. We can hang up the posters two days before we start our juice bar.
Anything else?

Kerry Well, we need a name for our bar. Any good ideas?

Ralph What about "Shocking Smoothies"?

Alex Great.

1 Smoothies at school

banana, glass, milk, poster, money, strawberry, office of the head master, juice bar

Lerntipp	Übertrage folgende Tabelle in dein Lernheft und ergänze eigene Sätze oder suche Sätze aus den vorhergehenden Units.		
hat in der **Vergangenheit** stattgefunden: **simple past:** play ▸ play**ed** / **didn't** play go ▸ went / didn't go	ist ein Zustand im Moment oder findet **regelmäßig** statt: **simple present** he, she, it – das S muss mit I play – he play**s**		wird erst in der **Zukunft** stattfinden: **will-future** will + Infinitiv (Grundform)
Yesterday I played football.	I have a cold. He listens to music every day.		Maybe my grandmother will come tomorrow.

SPEAKING

School paramedics

🎧 13 **Now you**

Bessy Who are the new school paramedics and what years are they from?
You We are eight students, four girls and four boys, we are from Year 7–9. (2P)
Bessy Who did the training with you?
You Two Essen paramedics, Susie and Martin, did the training with us. (2P)
Bessy When was the training and what did you learn?
You It was every Tuesday afternoon. We learned a lot about the work of paramedics. And we learned what we can do and when we must call the Essen paramedics. (5P)
Bessy How can the school paramedics help?
You We can help when there is somebody hurt or doesn't feel well. (3P)
Bessy When and where can students find you?
You There are always two of us in the school hall in every break and at lunch time. (3P)

| **Lerntipp** | Zum Überprüfen deiner Antworten kannst du sie entweder aufschreiben oder dich aufnehmen. Vergleiche dann mit den Lösungen im Lösungsheft. |

3 WORDS At the doctor's

1 Mr Miller has a headache.
2 John has a temperature.
3 Sally has a toothache.
4 Mr Baker has a stomach ache.
5 Susan has a cold.
6 Mrs Murple has an earache.

4 GRAMMAR Mum and Dad have got a lot of questions

2 Has the driver of the car written you an e-mail / visited you?
3 Has the doctor seen you?
4 Has your teacher written you an e-mail / visited you / brought you the homework?
5 Have your friends brought you the homework / written you an e-mail / visited you?
6 Have you read the new book?

5 GRAMMAR Where will they be when?

1 Natale will be at the police station next Monday.
2 Isabel will be in hospital tomorrow.
3 Barry will be at a football match next weekend.
4 Tracy and Terry will be at school in the afternoon.
5 Adam will be at home in a few minutes.

> **Lerntipp** Place before time
>
> Suche dir aus dem Text **Friday Dinner** auf S. 60 im Englischbuch die drei Sätze heraus, in denen eine Orts- **und** eine Zeitangabe vorkommen. Schreibe jeden Satz mit einer anderen Farbe ab.
> Schneide anschließend die Sätze auseinander und versuche sie wieder richtig zusammenzusetzen.

WRITING

Mike's letter to his grandma

Dear Grandma, (0,5)

Last Wednesday I went to school by bike. (1) I had an accident with a car on John's Street. (1). I fell and was unconscious. (1) The paramedics came very quickly and took me to hospital (2). I have a terrible headache and my left arm is broken (1,5). So I must stay in hospital for five days. (1) But it is not so boring. (1). Mum and Dad visit me every day and my friends from school brought CDs and a CD-player. (3)

I'm happy because I can go home tomorrow. (1)

Love Mike (0,5)

Lerntipp	So kannst du **Listening Skills** üben:

Höre dir den Text abschnittweise an und löse die jeweilige Aufgabe dazu.
Ganz schwierige Sätze kannst du auch öfter anhören und versuchen nachzusprechen.
Du verstehst dann den Sinn besser.

LANGUAGE

1 WORDS irregular verbs

Infinitive	Simple past form	Past participle	German translation
(to) be	was/were	been	sein
(to) eat	ate	eaten	essen
(to) find	found	found	finden
(to) go	went	gone	gehen
(to) come	came	come	kommen
(to) have	had	had	haben, besitzen
(to) take	took	taken	nehmen
(to) make	made	made	machen
(to) do	did	done	tun, machen
(to) see	saw	seen	sehen

2 GRAMMAR After the accident

1 Alan has already phoned the police. (1,5)
2 The paramedics have just taken the boy to hospital. (1,5)
3 Two policemen have already talked to the man. (1,5)
4 The policemen haven't written the report yet. (1,5)
5 The driver of the car hasn't visited the boy in hospital yet. (1,5)
6 The policemen have just phoned the boy's parents. (1,5)

Lerntipp	Übertrage die Tabelle in dein Lernheft und ergänze sie mit weiteren Beispielen aus Unit 4.

Adverbien der unbestimmten Zeit	
Adverb vor dem past participle: already • always • just • never often • ever	**Adverb am Satzende:** yet
I've **already** parked the car.	Dan hasn't come down **yet**.

Lösungen B

LISTENING

🎧 11 Three reports on an accident

The boy's story:

"Well, it happened on my way to school this morning. It was about 7.30 and still dark – so I had my lights on. There was a lot of traffic and rain, so I had my yellow rain cape on. You see, I was a bit late and I didn't want to be late for school, so I tried to be really quick. I wanted to ride into High Street. I looked out for cars or bikes. I was sure that there was no car or bike coming from the right … but then suddenly there was this black car. The car came very quickly. So, as I said, there was this black car and bang … I rode into it with my bike. Well, I fell to the ground and from that moment I can't remember anything. I woke up in hospital with a broken leg."

The woman's story:

"I feel better now, but it was a shock really. Anyway, I was going along High Street with my car. I drove carefully and really slowly because of the many schoolchildren, you know, when suddenly this bike came from the left. I couldn't see it because the lights of the bike weren't on. The boy had dark clothes on. He was very quick and drove into my car. Oh dear, I thought, and I stopped the car as quickly as possible. As I said, it was a shock for me. So I'm glad that a girl called the police and the paramedics."

The man's story:

"Well, I was in my car going along High Street. I was behind a black car. I must say, that the black car drove very fast, too fast, if you ask me. And then I saw this bike coming really fast, it was very quick. The boy had dark clothes on but I could see him, because the lights on his bike were on. As I said – the car was too fast and the bike was fast too. So … the accident happened. The boy fell off the bike to the ground and didn't move. I think he had a broken leg. So I called the police and the paramedics."

1 About the accident

boy – bike – was a bit late   **woman** – black car – has a shock   **man** – white car – called the police

2 More facts about the accident

	The boy's story	The woman's story	The man's story
lights on the boy's bike: yes/no?	yes	no	yes
the boy's bike: slow/fast?	fast	fast	fast
the boy's clothes	yellow rain cape	dark clothes	dark clothes
the woman's car: fast/slow?	fast	slow	fast
the boy's injuries	broken leg	✗	broken leg
Who called the paramedics?	✗	girl	he/man

Unit 4 | Lösungen A

MEDIATION

Where can we go?

Your mum	Sag ihr bitte, dass wir hier auf dem Campingplatz wohnen und gerne einige Tagesausflüge planen möchten. Frag sie dann bitte, ob sie uns ein paar Tipps geben kann.
You	Good morning. We are staying here at the camping site. We would like to plan some day trips. Could you help us, please? (2)
Woman	Yes, of course. There are many things to do here. But first let me ask you: Do you want to visit museums or do you want to go to our famous beaches?
You	Sie sagt, dass es hier eine Menge zu tun gibt. Sie möchte wissen, ob wir Museen besuchen möchten oder ob wir an die berühmten Strände gehen wollen. (2)
Your mum	Das ist schwierig zu beantworten. Wenn die Sonne scheint und es warm ist, gehen wir an die Strände. Aber wir brauchen auch Ideen für schlechtes Wetter. Wir könnten in ein oder zwei Museen gehen, finde ich.
You	Well, it's difficult to answer. If the sun shines and it's warm, then we will go to the beaches. But we need some ideas for bad weather, too. Then we would like to visit one or two museums. (3)
Woman	OK. I understand. On this map here you can see all the beaches near the camping site. I mark these two nice beaches for you on the map. You will like them.
You	Also, auf dieser Karte hier sieht man alle Strände in der Nähe unseres Campingplatzes. Sie markiert diese zwei schönen Strände für uns und sagt, dass sie uns gefallen werden. (3)
Woman	Now, if the weather is bad, there are many small museums. Here is a brochure with all the information.
You	Für schlechtes Wetter gibt es viele kleine Museen. Sie gibt uns eine Broschüre / ein Prospekt mit allen Informationen. / Hier ist eine Broschüre / ein Prospekt mit allen Informationen. (2)
Your mum	Das sind ja tolle Ideen. Bedank dich bitte und frag noch gleich nach einem guten Café.
You	My mum likes the ideas very much. Thank you very much. Is there a good café? (2)
Woman	Yes, you can go to the Red Dragon. That's very good. Bye-bye and have nice trips.
Your mum	Also, das habe ich jetzt auch verstanden. Thank you very much and bye-bye.

Unit 4 | Lösungen A

3 WORDS Opposites

a) (3P)

1 husband ◄► wife
2 strong ◄► weak
3 dirty ◄► clean

4 quiet ◄► noisy
5 valley ◄► mountains
6 exciting ◄► boring

b) Mögliche Lösungen (3P)

big ◄► small/little   good ◄► bad   hot ◄► cold

at the bottom (of) ◄► at the top (of)   fast ◄► slow

> **Lerntipp** So kannst du dir **Wörter gut merken**:
>
> ■ Du kannst dir Wörter besser merken, wenn du sie in Wortgruppen sammelst, z. B. als **Gegensatzpaare (opposites)**. Im Vocabulary deines Englischbuches findest du das Symbol ◄►. Es weist dich darauf hin, dass es sich um ein Gegensatzpaar handelt. Schreibe alle Gegensatzpaare aus den vergangenen Units in dein Lernheft.
>
> ■ Mehr Ideen zum Wörterlernen findest du im **Skills File Learning words – Step 2** auf S. 121 in deinem Englischbuch. Lies dort noch einmal nach.

4 STUDY SKILLS How to give a good presentation

a) (3P)

♣: 1 B, 2 C, 3 D, 4 A   ♦: 1 C, 2 B, 3 D, 4 A   ♠: 1 D, 2 B, 3 A, 4 C

b) (3P)

♣ = 2   ♦ = 1   ♠ = 3

♣ A good presentation needs good preparation. Before you start talking, prepare everything you need. Hang up posters, get the projector ready. Then wait till everybody is quiet.

♦ First you must say what you are talking about. Then start with your information. Don't read out your text. You should only have a few key words on your cards.

♠ Look at your listeners as often as you can. When you show pictures, you must always explain them. At the end of the presentation you should say that you have finished. Then ask for questions.

> **Lerntipp** So kannst du üben, **Sätze zu ordnen**:
>
> ■ Schreibe den Text aus der Übung ab und schneide ihn in Sätze auseinander. Jetzt kannst du versuchen, sie richtig anzuordnen. Schiebe sie einfach so lange hin und her bis du glaubst, dass du die richtige Reihenfolge gefunden hast. Dieses Verfahren kannst du immer anwenden, wenn du Sätze ordnen willst.
>
> ■ Um dich noch besser auf die Klassenarbeit vorzubereiten, kannst du jetzt die Aufgabe für das Dossier im Englischbuch auf S. 65 machen.

Lerntipp So bildest du das **present perfect**:

I
you
they *(Simon and Paul)*
we *(my friend and I)*
} + have/haven't + 3. Form (unregelmäßig oder regelmäßig)

he *(Mr Brown, Gareth)*
she *(Mrs Evans, Melinda)*
it *(the weather, the car)*
} + has/hasn't + 3. Form (unregelmäßig oder regelmäßig)

Diese Regel wird in der Zeichnung noch einmal bildlich dargestellt:

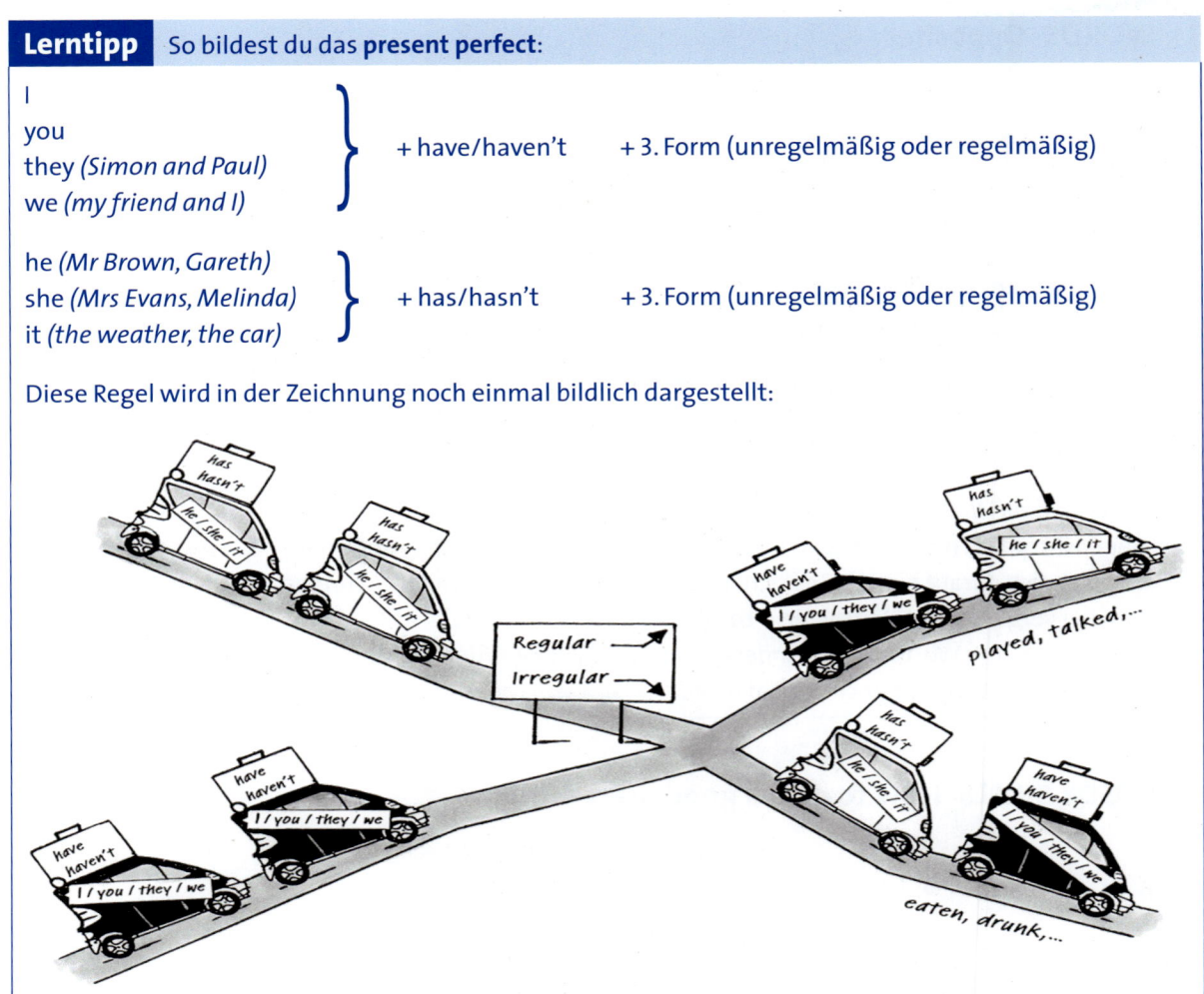

2 WORDS Describing a picture

a)

1 mountains, 2 valley, 3 fields, 4 cows, 5 river, 6 farm, 7 forest, 8 hills (4P)

b)

The picture is in the country. / shows the country. (1)

In the foreground there are cows. (1) They are standing next to a river. (1)

In the middle on the left there is a farm. (1) Behind the farm there are fields and a forest. (1)

In the background there are hills. (1) Behind the hills there are high mountains. (1)

On the mountains there is snow. (1) Between the mountains and the hills there is a valley. (1)

Lerntipp So kannst du **Describing pictures** üben: Wähle aus:

- Lies noch einmal das **Skills File Describing pictures** auf S.123 in deinem Englischbuch und beschreibe das Foto auf der Seite.
- Suche in deinem Lernheft den Abschnitt über **Describing pictures** heraus. Beschreibe das eingeklebte Bild ein zweites Mal schriftlich und vergleiche mit deiner ersten Lösung im Lernheft.
- Arbeite mit jemandem aus deiner Klasse zusammen: Du beschreibst ein beliebiges Bild aus deinem Englischbuch und dein Partner / deine Partnerin muss es finden: *It's at the top of page …*

Unit 4 — Lösungen A

READING

BBC Wales Bus on tour

1 The BBC Wales Bus and the students

In der Spalte "What did they do?" genügt es, wenn du zwei Aktivitäten angegeben hast, um die volle Punktzahl zu erhalten.

	Year 5	Year 6	Year 7	Everybody
When?	• Monday morning	• Monday afternoon	• Tuesday morning	• Tuesday afternoon
What was their topic?	• my way to school	• presentation	• trip to Cardiff	• open for everybody
What did they do?	• found out information about the way to school • made maps on the computer • reported to the other students	• practised with cameras • watched the films • talked about the presentations	• surfed the internet for information • collected ideas for a day trip to Cardiff • printed out the train times • found out about the train time / how much the return ticket is	• could ask for their favourite music

2 After the visit to the BBC Bus

Megan: 4, 5, 8   David: 1, 3, 6   Abby: 2, 7, 9

LANGUAGE

1 GRAMMAR What have they just done?

a)

1 Caroline has just written an e-mail.

2 Anna and Jenny have just found information about Caerphilly Castle.

3 Martin has just looked at the timetable.

4 Sue has just read about a museum in Cardiff.

b) Mögliche Lösungen:

I haven't done my homework yet.

I haven't tidied my room.

I have already helped my mum in the kitchen.

Unit 3 | Lösungen B

SPEAKING

🎧 10 An interview about pets

Mögliche Lösung:

your pet: (1P)	dog
he/she, name? (1P)	she, Lissi
what's special? (3 items) (3P)	– runs around in the garden, – likes playing with her red ball, – sits under my desk when I do my homework
who feeds / what food? (2P)	my sister, I / meat
parents: help? (2 items) (2P)	yes, go for walks, buy the food
holidays? (1P)	Lissi with us

Presenter Welcome to Bristol Today, the radio programme for families.
Tell me what pet have you got?

Alan I've got a dog.

Presenter Is it a he or a she and what's its name?

Alan Well, first it's a she and her name is Lissi.

Presenter Oh, that's a nice name. What is special about your pet?

Alan Well, Lissi runs around in the garden and likes playing with her ball.
She sits under my desk when I do my homework.

Presenter I see. Who feeds your pet and what food is best?

Alan Well, my sister and I feed her. The best food is meat.

Presenter What about your parents? Do they help you with your pet and what do they do?

Alan Yes, they do. They go for walks with her and buy the food for her.

Presenter One more question: what do you do when you go on holiday?

Alan Oh, Lissi goes on holiday with us, of course.

Lerntipp So kannst du **Speaking Skills** üben:

- Höre dir den Dialog zwischen Alan und dem Moderator noch einmal an.
- Sprich Alans Antworten laut nach. Achte auf seine Aussprache und die Satzmelodie und versuche sie zu imitieren.
- Sprich dann deine eigenen Antworten und achte auf die Satzmelodie.
- Achte besonders auf deine Antworten auf die Frage: What's special about your pet? Hier musst du deine eigenen Gedanken einbringen.

4 GRAMMAR My cat Minky

Minky is a nice cat. She sits quietly on my bed for hours. But if I don't give her a good lunch, she is angry and walks away quickly. She is very clever, too. If she sees a bird she will move slowly, so that the bird can't see her. When the bird flies away, Minky turns round angrily. Last year she had five sweet babies. She fed them carefully. After two months we gave them away to some good friends. I was so sad. But when I saw them play happily in my friends' garden it was OK.

> **Lerntipp** So kannst du **Adjektive / Adverbien** gut üben:
> - Lies das **Grammar File** auf S. 139 in deinem Englischbuch.
> - Überlege noch einmal, wann du Adjektive und wann du Adverbien verwenden musst. Schreibe deine Lösung auf und vergleiche sie mit dem **Grammar File** auf S. 139.
> - Schreibe regelmäßige und unregelmäßige Formen der Adverbien in dein Lernheft.

5 GRAMMAR My dog Norah

Mögliche Lösungen:

1 She runs quickly.
2 She does tricks very well.
3 She says hello very happily.
4 She brings the newspaper very carefully.

MEDIATION

Finding out about Animal Helpline

1 Sie sind eine Organisation für Tiere. Sie lieben Tiere und wollen Tierquälerei beenden. / Sie finden eine neues Zuhause für viele Tiere. (2P)

2 Nein, von der Regierung bekommen sie überhaupt kein Geld. Sie bekommen alles von den Leuten (der Bevölkerung). (2P)

3 Sie kommen zum Tierheim und helfen mit den Tieren. (1P)

4 Sie machen jedes Jahr im Juni einen Sponsorenlauf. Da bekommen sie sehr viel Geld zusammen. Letztes Jahr liefen über 800 Menschen mehr als 4000 Meilen. (3P)

5 Sie können etwas von ihrem Taschengeld abgeben. (1P)

6 Sie hat im Jahr 2007 in einer Lotterie gewonnen und der Organisation £1000 gegeben! (2P)

7 Die Helpline ist dann wichtig, wenn man Tierquälerei melden möchte. (1P)

> **Lerntipp** So kannst du **Mediation** gut üben:
> - Lies den Text mehrmals laut vor.
> - Lies die Fragen, die du aus dem Text beantworten sollst.
> - Benutze einen Markierstift und markiere dir die wichtigen Textpassagen.
> - Beantworte dann die Fragen.

2 WORDS Say it in English

Was sagst du, wenn du …

1 … jemand darauf aufmerksam machen möchtest, dass er frieren wird? <u>You will be cold.</u>
2 … eine Übung nicht schwierig findest? <u>This exercise isn't hard.</u>
3 … möchtest, dass jemand etwas aufhebt? <u>Pick it up, please.</u>
4 … jemanden bittest, dir etwas zu erklären? <u>Can you explain that to me?</u>
5 … bedauerst, dass du gehen musst? <u>I have to go now, I'm afraid.</u>
6 … jemanden bittest, das Eis kühl zu halten? <u>Keep the ice cream cool.</u>

3 GRAMMAR In the pet shop

Mrs Brother	Now Gillian, let's look at all the pets.
Gillian	Well, Mum. If I <u>take</u> (take) a dog, I will have to go for a walk every morning.
Mrs Brother	Yes, that's right, dear. But if you get up a bit earlier every morning, this <u>will not be</u> (not be) a problem.
Gillian	Hm, I don't know. What about a cat, Mum?
Mrs Brother	Well, if you buy a cat, things <u>will be</u> (be) easier.
Gillian	You're right. But what can we do if our cat <u>runs</u> (run) on the road?
Mrs Brother	Yes, that's another big problem. What about a budgie?
Gillian	OK, Mum. I think I'll have the budgie.
Mrs Brother	If you want a budgie, you <u>must clean</u> (clean) the cage. OK?

Lerntipp Conditional sentences type 1 (Bedingungssätze Typ 1)

- Lies im Englischbuch noch einmal die Regeln für die Bedingungssätze im **Grammar File** auf S. 138.
- Füge dann die Regeln und Beispielsätze aus dem Gedächtnis in den Kasten ein.
- Überprüfe das Geschriebene und übertrage es in dein Lernheft.

if – Satz (Bedingung)	Hauptsatz (Folge für die Zukunft)

Unit 3 — Lösungen B

READING

1 About the pets

cat: ball – bowl of water – sofa   **dog**: bowl of water – dog classes   **guinea pig**: bottle of water – hay (Heu)

2 What do you know about the pets?

	guinea pig	cat	dog
1 It's better to have more than one of them.	✔		
2 You must spend a lot of money on this pet in one year.			✔
3 It likes the garden.	✔	✔	✔
4 It needs a bed.	✔		
5 It wants to go for a walk with you.			✔
6 You can teach it.			✔
7 It likes sleeping.		✔	
8 This pet likes to be alone.		✔	
9 Be friendly to this pet – or it will not be friendly to you.		✔	
10 Don't leave this pet alone the whole day.			✔
11 This pet doesn't like the sun.	✔		

> **Lerntipp** So kannst du **Reading Skills** üben:
> - Wähle einen der drei Texte aus.
> - Erstelle eine Mindmap oder eine Tabelle für den ausgewählten Text: Überlege dir sinnvolle Oberbegriffe, z. B activities/what is special about them/…
> - Schreibe dann die wichtigsten Informationen zu den jeweiligen Oberbegriffen dazu.
> - Die so übersichtlich geordneten Informationen helfen dir anschließend bei den Lösungen.

LANGUAGE

1 WORDS Find the words.

1 The children are playing <u>in the yard</u>.
2 Tonight the <u>moon</u> is beautiful.
3 What a lot of <u>rubbish</u>!
4 Sandra is in the <u>clinic</u>. Paul is <u>visiting</u> her.
5 Liam and Peter want to make a <u>fire</u>.
6 Last month we <u>moved</u> to London.
7 Oh <u>dear</u>! The window is <u>broken</u>.
8 Your room must always look <u>neat and tidy</u>.

3 GRAMMAR What will life be like in 20 years?

1 In twenty years people will have fast and safe cars.
2 In twenty years students won't have teachers. They will have computers only. (2 P)
3 In twenty years there will be no more shops in small villages.
4 In twenty years people will buy everything on the internet.

4 GRAMMAR What Josh will do if he gets a dog:

1 If my parents buy a dog for me, I will work hard for school. / …, I will always tidy my room. / …
2 I'll call her Lulu if it is a she.
3 If the weather is nice, I will play in the garden with her. / …, I will go out for walks with her. / …
4 I'll take Lulu to the animal clinic if she is ill. / … if she is hurt. / …
5 I'll help in the kitchen if I have a dog. / … if my parents buy a dog for me. / …
6 If my friends come to my house, we will play with Lulu. / … will teach Lulu tricks. / …

> **Lerntipp** Die Struktur der **Bedingungssätze Typ 1 (conditional sentences type 1)** lässt sich mit folgender Übung leicht einprägen. Du kannst sie mündlich oder schriftlich machen.

Nimm diese Aussage von Josh als Ausgangssatz: *I'll be happy if my parents buy a dog for me.*
Ergänze ihn bei jedem erneuten Sagen oder Aufschreiben um ein bis drei Worte.
Das können auch humorvolle Ergänzungen sein, z. B.

1. I will be **really** happy if my parents buy a dog for me.
2. I will be **really** happy if my parents buy a **little green** dog for me.
3. …

Wie viele Ergänzungen schaffst du?

Lerne den Ausgangssatz auswendig. In der Klassenarbeit kannst du dir den Satz gut in Erinnerung zurückrufen und hast so ein Beispiel mit der richtigen Struktur:
Hauptsatz: **will-future** – if-Satz: **simple present**.

WRITING

A letter to Ian

Bristol, 1st June

Dear Ian,

I went to a fun run last week. I think a fun run is a good idea because it is really fun and you can help to collect money. (2P) This fun run was for the 'Animal Helpline' here in Bristol. (1P) My sponsors were my parents. (1P) I told them about the fun run and about 'Animal Helpline' and their work. (1P) They paid £1 for each mile that I ran. (1P) I ran together with my friends from school (1P) and we ran 21 miles together. Not bad. (1P) We had a lot of fun. The best thing about the fun run was that there were old and young people. They all wanted to help 'Animal Helpline'. With every mile we helped an animal. That's great, I think.
If there is another fun run next year, I will tell you before. Perhaps you can come too. OK? (2P)
Lots of love / See you soon (1P)

Unit 3 | Lösungen A

1 Pets and people

Mrs Hall – dog – Noodle

Mary – budgie – Mr Bean

Mrs Gray – cat – Mousy

Josh – dog – ??

2 About the radio programme

In today's radio programme … a), b)

Mrs Hall … a)

Mary … b), c)

Mrs Gray … b)

Josh … b), c)

> **Lerntipp** So kannst du **Listening Skills** üben:
>
> ■ Höre dir den Text an und lies laut mit. Du findest den Text in den Lösungen auf S. 21.
> ■ Lerne einzelne Teile des Textes auswendig und sprich sie frei nach.

LANGUAGE

1 WORDS When you go on holiday

1 When you want to go on holiday you pack your clothes in a suitcase.
2 When you want to go by train and come back too you need a return ticket.
3 When you want to go on holiday and you have got a pet it's important that somebody looks after your pet.
4 The opposite of happy is sad.
5 The opposite of friend is enemy.
6 If you are ill you can't go to school.
7 This bird lives in a tree: woodpecker.
8 If you promise to do something you will do it and you must do it.
9 If you like somebody very much you can call him or her your sweetheart.

> **Lerntipp** So kannst du **Vokabeln** üben:
>
> ■ Nimm dir zehn Wörter aus der Unit vor, die dir nicht so leicht fallen.
> ■ Gib jedem Wort eine Farbe, die dir spontan dazu einfällt. Notiere dir das Wort mit Übersetzung und setze dahinter mit einem Buntstift einen Farbklecks.
> ■ Halte dann das Wort zu, sodass du nur noch die Farbe siehst und versuche dich nun aus dem Gedächtnis an das Wort und seine Übersetzung zu erinnern.

2 WORDS Who is at the animal party?

1 There are three foxes. (0,5)
2 There is one lion. (0,5)
3 There are two deer. (0,5)
4 There are three frogs. (0,5)
5 There is one hedgehog. (1)
6 There are two crocodiles. (1)
7 There is one woodpecker. (1)
8 There are two squirrels. (1)
9 There is one mole. (1)
10 There are two wolves. (1)

Lösungen A

LISTENING

🎧 08 Pets in Bristol

Presenter Hello, everybody. Welcome to Bristol Today, the radio programme for families. This afternoon we want to talk about your pets: Who in your family has got a pet? Who feeds it? Have you got any problems with your pet? These are only some of the questions that we would like to hear about from you. So, come on, everybody. I'm waiting for your call.

The telephone rings.

Presenter Oh, that was quick. Bristol Today, hello.
Mrs Hall Hello, this is Susan Hall speaking. I've got a nice little dog; his name is Noodle and he's about seven years old.
Presenter Well, this sounds very nice. And who in your family feeds Noodle and who goes for walks with him?
Mrs Hall You see, I live alone. So I feed him, of course. And we love to go for long walks in the park together. But the problem is that I hurt my leg last week and so at the moment I can't walk.
Presenter So, who goes for a walk with Noodle now?
Mrs Hall My neighbour does at the moment. She is very nice. But she will be on holiday next week. So I don't know what to do, really.
Presenter Now, Mrs Hall, I understand your problem. If we are lucky we can find somebody for you this afternoon. So thank you for calling. Bye-bye.

(blip)

Oh, here is our next listener already, hello, who is calling?
Mary Hello, this is Mary from Bristol.
Presenter Hello Mary. Tell us, what pet have you got?
Mary I've got a budgie, his name is Mr Bean.
Presenter What a funny name!! Now Mary, we would like to know: do you always clean Mr Bean's cage?
Mary Well, I do whenever I can. But sometimes when there is a lot to do for school, my mum does it. But then I help her in the kitchen on another day.
Presenter OK Mary. Thanks a lot for calling.

(blip)

Bristol Today, hello. Who am I talking to?
Mrs Gray Hello, my name is Mrs Gray, Sandra Gray.
Presenter Well Mrs Gray, what pet have you got?
Mrs Gray I don't have my *own* pet, my neighbours and I have a black cat together. Her name is Mousy. She is in my house and in my garden all day when my neighbours are out. In the evening Mousy goes to my neighbours' house. We are all really good friends.
Presenter Now this is really interesting. Thanks for calling, Mrs Gray.

(blip)

And here is our last listener before we have some more music. Bristol Today, hello.
Josh Hi, my name is Josh. And I'm 13 years old.
Presenter Hello Josh. You want to tell us something about your pet, do you?
Josh Yes and no. I would love to have a dog but my mum and dad won't let me have one. They say that I don't have enough time for a dog, because I'm still at school.
Presenter I understand. But Josh, I've got an idea – why don't you call Mrs Hall and ask her if you can go for walks with her dog Noodle? You remember she hurt her leg. I'll give you her number in a minute. But first, let's have some music. Here is …

Unit 2 | Lösungen B

WRITING

An article for the school magazine

I'm writing about our school project. Our topic was the school garden. (1) We did this project because the old garden was not nice. (2) But we had no money for the flowers. (2) So we baked cakes and sold them at school and at Bristol Market. (2) We needed help with our school garden and got it from Mr Hull from the flower shop. (3) Our parents helped us, too. (1) At the end of the project we did a presentation for our parents. (2) We invited our parents to some cakes and drinks because we wanted to say thank you. (2)

> **Lerntipp** Lies noch einmal den Reading text *This year's fashion show – a hit* auf S. 21 im Aufgabenheft. Der Text ist ein ausführliches Beispiel für einen Artikel in der Schülerzeitung.

SPEAKING

🎧 07 Two countries – two projects

Sally Hi! I'm Sally, I'm from Bristol. I want to tell you something about our school garden project. What about you? What was your project about?

You Our project was about our classroom / a classroom project. (1)

Sally That's interesting. Let me tell you why we started our project. You see, we had this old school garden in our school. It looked awful. So one day we had the idea to make it nicer. But now tell me why you started your project.

You Well, our classroom was so awful and the lamps were very old. So one day we had the idea to paint it and to put up new lamps. (2)

Sally Good idea. Now, we really had a problem because we needed an expert and we needed money for the plants. What about your form, did you have any problems, too?

You Yes, of course. We needed help and we needed money, too. (1)

Sally We sold cakes at school and at the market in Bristol. How did you get the money for the project?

You We had a flea market with old books. / We got the money from a flea market with old books. (2)

Sally Good! When we had the money, we started working in the garden. It looks super now, really. How did you go on with your project and who helped you?

You We painted the classroom and put up new lamps. Our parents helped us. (2)

Sally At the end we presented the project to our parents and the teachers. What about your presentation?

You We presented the classroom project to our parents and the teachers too. (2)

> **Lerntipp** So kannst du **Speaking Skills** üben:
> - Höre dir Sallys Ausführungen einige Male an. Achte dabei auf ihre Aussprache und die Satzmelodie.
> - Sprich zunächst einfach nach, was Sally sagt. Drücke dazu einfach die Pausentaste, wenn Sally gesprochen hat.
> - Sprich erst nach dieser Übung deinen eigenen Teil. Benutze dazu die Bilder und deine eigenen Notizen.
> - Wenn du einen aufnahmefähigen MP3-Player oder ein Mikrofon am Computer hast, kannst du dich aufnehmen. Dann kannst du deine Antworten noch besser überprüfen.

Unit 2 | Lösungen B

> **Lerntipp** So kannst du **how much / how many** üben:
>
> - Erstelle in deinem Lernheft eine Tabelle und ordne die Fragen nach *How much* und *How many*.
> - Unterstreiche *How much* und das folgende Wort in einer bestimmten Farbe.
>   Verfahre bei *How many* und dem folgenden Wort genauso (z. B. *how much time* …).
> - Jetzt kannst du Folgendes erkennen:
>   – **wie viel** heißt auf Englisch **how much**
>   – **wie viele** heißt auf Englisch **how many**
> - Schreibe in deine Tabelle jeweils noch fünf weitere Beispiele
>   (z. B. *How many apples? How much snow?*)

2 WORDS Say it in English

1 What's the matter?
2 You're wrong.
3 I agree with you.
4 Shut up!
5 What are you doing?
6 Don't make a mess.

3 WORDS Opposites

1 expensive
2 worse
3 left/wrong
4 awful/terrible/bad
5 (to) start
6 exciting/interesting

7 slow
8 (to) spend money
9 (to) lose
10 bigger
11 stupid
12 (to) hate

4 GRAMMAR What they can buy

1 The apple cake is better than the cheese cake. The chocolate cake is the best.
2 The tree is more beautiful than the bush. The flower is the most beautiful.
3 The second bench is funnier than the first bench. The third bench is the funniest.
4 The first spade is cheaper than the second spade. The third spade is the cheapest.

5 GRAMMAR About yourself

2 In my class I'm the smallest / funniest / youngest / … student.
3 I'm younger/smaller/… than my aunt/uncle.
4 I'm as clever as/… my teacher.
5 I'm not as big as/… my cousin/brother/sister.

Unit 2 — Lösungen B

LISTENING

🎧 06 Presentation of a project

Mike Good evening, ladies and gentlemen, hello boys and girls, I'm Mike from 7 DH. Today we – the students of form 7 DH – want to welcome you to our presentation of the project 'Our school garden'. There are three parts to our presentation: first we want to show you how we got the idea for our project, our second point is to tell you something about the work of the different groups, and at the end we want to invite you to try our home-made cakes and have something to drink. But now please listen to Sally.

Sally OK, I'm telling you about the idea. The school garden wasn't nice because nobody worked there. In summer we often played outside so we saw the old garden and one day we talked about it. That was the start of the idea. We wanted to make the garden nice again. So we talked to our form teacher Mrs Wallace. She liked our idea. The second important person was the head teacher Mrs Bloom. When she agreed our project could start. There were two things: we wanted to make the garden nice with flowers from April to October and we wanted to have some benches to sit on.

Carol Hello everybody, I'm Carol. Well, the first thing that we had to do was to plan the garden. But nobody knew how to plan a garden. So we needed experts. Mr Hull from the flower shop here in Bristol is a really good expert and he helped us a lot. The next problem was that we had no money. So we made cakes and the other students bought our cakes in the school breaks. Then we sold the cakes at Bristol Market too because everybody said that they were so good. We made quite a lot of money. The different groups worked with this money: they bought flowers and plants. Many fathers and mothers helped us too. We want to say thank you for your help.

Mike Well, we hope you liked our presentation. Now let's go into the garden for some cakes and a drink. Come on, everybody …

1 The project

(1) D, (2) C, (3) F, (4) B, (5) H, (6) A, (7) E, (8) G

2 HEADS AND TAILS About the school garden

1d), 2e), 3i), 4f), 5b), 6g), 7c)

LANGUAGE

1 GRAMMAR Questions about the project

1 <u>How much</u> time did you have for the project?
2 <u>How many</u> parents helped you with the project?
3 <u>How much</u> money did you need for the plants?
4 <u>How many</u> cakes did you make?
5 <u>How much</u> sugar did you need for all the cakes?
6 <u>How many</u> students worked in the presentation group?

MEDIATION

Preparing the show

Jessica	Was geschieht hier?
You	Jessica wants to know what is happening here.
Lucy	We're preparing our fashion show.
You	Lucy sagt, sie bereiten eine Modenschau vor. (1)
Jessica	Frag sie bitte, wer die Modenschau präsentiert.
You	Jessica wants to know who presents the fashion show. (1)
Lucy	Every year the boys and girls of the forms 8, 9 and 10 present it.
You	Sie sagt, dass das jedes Jahr die Jungen und Mädchen der Klassen 8, 9 und 10 machen. (1)
Jessica	Ist eine Modenschau jedes Jahr nicht langweilig?
You	She wants to know if (ob) a fashion show every year isn't boring. (1)
Lucy	Sometimes yes. But this year every form has a different topic, so it can't be boring.
You	Sie sagt, dass es manchmal schon langweilig sein kann. / Manchmal schon. Aber dieses Jahr hat jede Klasse ein anderes Thema, also kann es nicht langweilig werden. (2)
Jessica	Und wann ist die Modenschau? Ich möchte gerne kommen.
You	And when is the fashion show? She wants to come. (2)
Lucy	Great. It's on Saturday evening.
You	Sie freut sich und sagt, dass es am Samstagabend ist. / Großartig. Sie findet am Samstagabend statt. (2)

> **Lerntipp** So kannst du **Mediations-Aufgaben** üben:
>
> ▪ Versuche, dich in die Personen hineinzudenken, für die du vermittelst. Du sprichst also nicht für dich selber, sondern abwechselnd für den einen oder den anderen Gesprächspartner.
> ▪ Lies dir noch einmal die vorgeschlagenen Lösungen durch und überprüfe vor allem auch, ob du bei deinen Lösungen die Veränderungen der Person richtig gemacht hast:
> z.B.: **We** are preparing our fashion show. ▶ **Sie** bereiten ...
> ▪ Lies dir in deinem Englischbuch auf S. 131 das **Skills File Mediation** durch.

Unit 2 | Lösungen A

Lerntipp	Die Steigerung der Adjektive	
Mit -er/-est	**Mit more / most**	**Unregelmäßig**
Einsilbige Adjektive: old – older – oldest **Adjektive auf -y:** happy – happier – happiest	**Andere zwei- und mehrsilbige Adjektive:** terrible – more terrible – most terrible	good – better – best

- Übertrage diese Tabelle sorgfältig in dein Lernheft und ergänze weitere Adjektive. Markiere in der linken Spalte alle Besonderheiten in der Schreibweise, z. B. hot – ho**tt**er – ho**tt**est oder happy – happ**i**er – happ**i**est
- Überprüfe deine zusätzlichen Einträge mithilfe des Grammar File auf den Seiten 135 und 136 in deinem Englischbuch.
- Bearbeite die Polly Aufgabe auf S. 136.

5 GRAMMAR Before the fashion show

Lucy Our show is a big surprise. What about the students of form 10 FR? Do you know anything about theirs?

Claire No, I don't. But I know that ours is great. Our hats are a super idea. My mum helped me with my hat, so mine is ready. What about yours, Lucy? Is your hat ready?

Lucy Well, mine is almost ready. Did you see Jenny's hat? Hers is super. Can I see yours now, Claire?

Claire So what do you think of my hat, Lucy?

Lucy Wow, yours is the best, really!

Lerntipp	Possessive pronouns (Possessivpronomen)

- Possessivpronomen werden verwendet, wenn ein bereits genanntes Nomen nicht noch einmal wiederholt werden soll: z.B. *Is this your pencil?* – Anstatt zu antworten: *No,* **my pencil** *is green.* sagt man besser: *No,* **mine** *is green.*
- Vervollständige diese Tabelle. Überprüfe sie anschließend mithilfe des Merkkastens auf S. 156 in deinem Englischbuch.

	Possessive pronoun	German translation
my pencil	mine	meiner (meine, meins)
your pencil		
his pencil		
her pencil		
(Dan and Joe:) your pencil		
their pencil		

LANGUAGE

1 WORDS What people said after the fashion show

Betty   I love fashion shows – they're fantastic. Luke was our presenter. He was great.

Susan   There were more than 600 people in the assembly hall! Everybody liked the fashion show!

Mr Hall   Why didn't you join me, Susan? The show was super.

John   I thought, oh no, not another boring fashion show. I was fed up with fashion shows. But this one was different.

Form teacher   Great idea, form 9TG – you used old stuff for new hats. A great example of recycling.

2 WORDS Clothes

Nouns: jacket, pullover, cap, skirt, trousers, a pair of trainers, dress, shirt, shorts, shoes, …

Verbs: wash, choose, clean, design, sell, wear, …

Adjectives: beautiful, awful, cheap, expensive, dark, nice, old, new, pretty, …

> **Lerntipp**   **Wortfelder** zur Wiederholung und Festigung von Vokabeln
>
> - Mit **Wortfeldern** kannst du dir Wörter besser merken.
> - Lies dazu das **Skills File 2 Learning words – Step 2** auf S. 121 in deinem Englischbuch.
> - Wiederhole nicht nur Substantive, sondern auch Verben und Adjektive.

3 GRAMMAR This year's fashion show

The fashion show was super!! The colours of the Indian clothes were more beautiful than the others. The music of form 8 HG was quieter than the music of the other forms. The hats of 9 TG were cheaper than the clothes of 8 HG and 10 FR. I think our school uniform can look funnier with one of the hats. But with a hat it is more expensive than at the moment. There were more topics than the years before. This year's fashion show was better than last year's show.

4 GRAMMAR What do you think?

Mögliche Lösungen:

1. skirt – trousers   I think trousers are nicer than skirts.
2. English – Maths   English is more difficult than Maths.
3. computer games – TV   Computer games are more exciting than TV.

Unit 2 — Lösungen A

READING

This year's fashion show – a hit

1 The fashion show

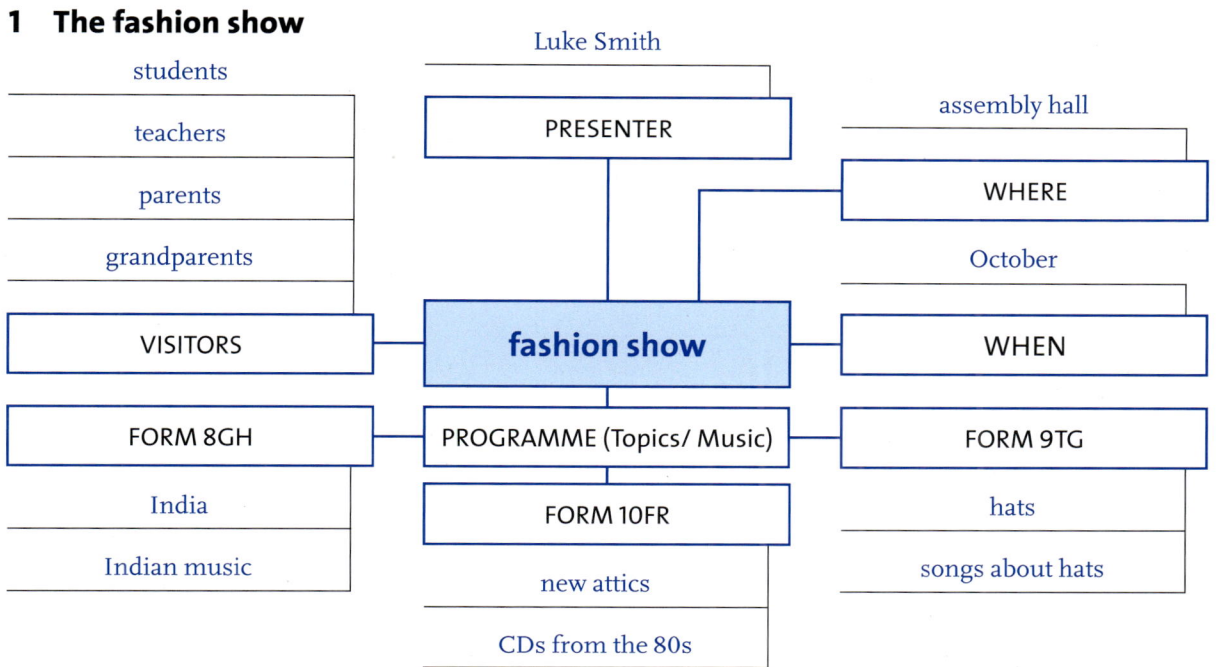

2 More about the fashion show

Für jede Zeile, in der du die Kreuze in die richtigen Kästchen gemacht hast, kannst du dir einen Punkt anrechnen.

The school	The models	Luke Smith	The show	Form 8 HG	Form 9 TG	Form 10 FR	The parents	The grandparents	The teachers	
				✔		✔				had music from a CD. (2)
			✔							was one of the best shows in the last years. (1)
		✔								explained why the name for the fashion of Form 10 FR was 'new attics'. (1)
					✔		✔	✔	✔	sang while the models presented. (4)
						✔				presented old-fashioned clothes. (1)
✔										has a fashion show every year. (1)
	✔	✔								was/were very nervous. (2)
				✔	✔	✔				had a topic for their show. (3)
				✔						presented fashion from another country. (1)
						✔				showed hats from recycled material. (1)

SPEAKING

🎧 05 Last Sunday

4 October   *Sunday*

8.00	got up at 8.30
9.00	had breakfast with Mum
10.00	played computer
11.00	went to a toy museum with Mum
12.00	had lunch at the café in the museum, went home
13.00	
14.00	did my homework
15.00	
16.00	watched football on TV
17.00	
18.00	went to Grandma with Mum, had tea
19.00	
20.00	went home, tidied my room, too late to watch TV
21.00	went to bed

Lösungsvorschlag:

I got up at 8.30 and had a long breakfast with Mum. (1,5 P) After that I played my new computer game. (1,5 P) At 11 o'clock Mum and I went to a museum. (1,5 P) We looked at old toys. I liked it very much. (1,5 P) We had lunch at the museum café and then we went home. (1,5 P) In the afternoon I learned English for the test next Wednesday, then I watched a football match on TV. (1,5 P) At 6 o'clock Mum and I went to Grandma and had tea there. (1,5 P) We went home at 8 o'clock. After that I tidied my room.(1,5 P) I didn't watch a film on TV, because it was too late. (1,5 P) I went to bed at 9 o'clock. (1,5 P)

> **Lerntipp**   So kannst du **Speaking Skills** üben:
> - Höre dir Sarahs Ausführungen noch zweimal ganz genau an.
> - Beim zweiten Durchgang kannst du immer nach einem Satz die Pausentaste drücken und den Satz nachsprechen.
> - Höre dann den gesamten Text noch einmal an.

5 WORDS Say it in English

1 Mind your own business.

2 No way!

3 Come on.

4 Do you really think so?

WRITING

An e-mail to Germany

Hi Kai,

Last week I started school again. We've got a new form teacher. His name is Mr Miller. (3 P) I liked the International Music Camp very much and I learned a lot there.(3) I would like to go to a music camp again.(2) What about you? Did you like the music camp, too? (2) Do you want to come / Would you like to come to Great Britain again? (2) Did you learn much English in Scotland? (2) What did you do in the last two weeks of your holidays? (2) Please tell me about your German school. (2)

Please write back soon.

See you soon.

Simon (2)

 Lies nochmal den Lerntipp auf S. 11 zu Nr. 3 Grammar: An interview.
Überprüfe deine Fragen. Hast du die Lerntipps beachtet?
Eine weitere Hilfe für dich sind auch die Postkarten im Englischbuch auf S. 6 und 7.

3 GRAMMAR An interview

George When did you come to this school?

Why did you want to be a teacher?

Did you go to school in Bristol?

Where did you stay in your last holiday?

What do you teach?

Do you like your job?

When do you get up in the morning?

What do you do in your free time?

Lerntipp So kannst du üben, Fragen im **simple present** und **simple past** zu bilden. Vervollständige die Fragen im Kasten unten. Übertrage den ausgefüllten Kasten in dein Lernheft.

Fragen mit **did / do** oder **does** ohne Fragewort

Did _____?
Do _____?
Does _____?

Fragen mit **did / do** oder **does** mit Fragewort

When did _____?
What do _____?
Where does _____?

4 WORDS Irregular verbs

Infinitive	Simple past form	German translation
1 hear	heard	hören
2 teach / throw	taught / threw	lehren / werfen
3 drink / drive	drank / drove	trinken / fahren
4 know / keep	knew / kept	wissen / halten
5 meet / make	met / made	treffen / machen
6 read / run	read / ran	lesen / rennen
7 speak / see	spoke / saw	sprechen / sehen
8 eat	ate	essen

Lerntipp So kannst du dir die **unregelmäßigen Verben** gut merken:
- Übe regelmäßig mit deinen Karteikarten.
- Stelle fest, wie viele unregelmäßige Verben du jetzt schon kannst und versuche sie aus dem Gedächtnis aufzuschreiben.
- Schreibe dann die fehlenden Verben in deine Liste dazu.

Unit 1 | Lösungen B

2 The children and their holidays

Right: Sarah: b), d)   Peter: c)   Jason: b)   Simon: a), d)   David: c), d)

> **Lerntipp** So kannst du **Listening Skills** üben:
> - Höre dir den Listening-Text zunächst ganz an.
> - Höre den Text beim zweiten Durchgang jeweils abschnittweise an.

LANGUAGE

1 GRAMMAR Lunch break at school

David My brother and I <u>were</u> at Bristol Summer Camp. It <u>was</u> great. What about you, where <u>were</u> you?

Susan My parents and I <u>were</u> in Spain. It <u>was</u> hot and sunny. We <u>weren't</u> there for long, only for 10 days.

Jeremy So, the weather <u>was</u> good in Spain. I <u>was</u> in Ireland. It <u>wasn't</u> hot and sunny there, it <u>was</u> very wet and windy.

> **Lerntipp** Schreibe dir die **simple past** Formen von **(to) be** übersichtlich in dein Lernheft (siehe Aufgabenteil S. 17).
> - Bilde mit jeder Person mindestens einen Satz.

2 GRAMMAR About the weekend

1 **Sally** <u>Where</u> did you go at the weekend, Charlie?
   Charlie I was in London.

2 **Sally** <u>Who</u> did you go with?
   Charlie I went with my aunt and uncle from Oxford.

3 **Sally** <u>Where</u> did you stay in London?
   Charlie We stayed at a big hotel outside London.

4 **Sally** <u>Why</u> did you stay outside London?
   Charlie Because it was not so expensive.

5 **Sally** <u>When</u> did you come back home from London?
   Charlie At 8 o'clock on Sunday evening.

6 **Sally** And ..., <u>what</u> do you think about London?
   Charlie Well, what a question, it was just great, great, great!!!

> **Lerntipp** So kannst du üben, das richtige **Fragewort** zu finden:
> - Vergleiche den unvollständigen Fragesatz mit der Antwort und überlege, wonach gefragt wird.
> - Wähle dann das richtige Fragewort aus.

Lösungen B

Unit 1

LISTENING

🎧 04 Bristol Today

Reporter   Hello, everybody. Welcome to Bristol Today, the radio programme for families. This afternoon we are interviewing young people about their holidays for the last time. Well, today we have five young visitors. They spent their holidays at different places. But they were all at summer camps. Hello, Sarah. Please tell us about your holidays and about your camp.

Sarah   Well, I like riding, so I went to a horse camp in Cornwall. It was great to be together with the horses all day. In the mornings we cleaned the horses and in the afternoons we went on riding tours in the country. I was there for one week only. I liked it so much that I want to go for two weeks next year.

Reporter   Thank you Sarah. Our next guest is Peter. Peter, you were at a camp with a funny name.

Peter   Yes, that's right. I was at "Abracadoodle Summer Camp". We learned everything about the circus. I learned to do lots of magic tricks. At the end of the week we had a great show. Our families and friends came and were very amazed at what we had learned at the camp.

Reporter   Well, Peter, we can hear from what you say that you had a lot of fun. Now, what about you, Jason? What did you do?

Jason   Well, my hobby is football. So my dream was a football camp in the summer holidays. I went to Southampton and stayed there for three weeks. Of course there were no girls, just about 35 boys who wanted to play football all day long. I thought I was good at football, but I'm much better now. We played every morning and every afternoon. And I can say: I learned lots of new things in these three weeks.

Reporter   Thank you very much, Jason. You have a different hobby, Simon. Please tell us what you did, Simon.

Simon   Yes, thank you, I play the guitar, so when I heard of this international music camp in Scotland I knew that this was for me. It was very expensive, but my parents said yes, so I went to Scotland for one week. We stayed in a school – yes in a school – but I liked it very much. We had nice rooms. There were always four boys or four girls in one room. We also helped in the kitchen. There were boys and girls from Germany, Spain and Britain. We had a lot of fun and at the end we presented a musical.

Reporter   Thank you, Simon. Now, let's listen to our last guest. Hello, David. Now David, what was special about your camp?

David   Well, it was called Bristol Summer Camp – and – yes, it was here in Bristol. So my brother Ben and I stayed at home and for two weeks we went to the camp every morning. We did different things. We worked on a pirate ship, read stories about pirates, went on bike trips and of course had a lot of fun. One day we even made our own radio programme here at Radio Bristol.

Reporter   Yes, your show was at the end of the holidays, and … I must say: I liked it very much. Well, ladies and gentlemen, boys and girls, we are at the end of our programme for today. Thanks a lot to our young friends here in the studio. Bye-bye.

1 At the summer camps

Sarah: 1 week, riding camp

Peter: 1 week, circus camp

Jason: 3 weeks, football camp

Simon: 1 week, music camp

David: 2 weeks, Bristol Summer Camp

MEDIATION

David helps his brother Ben

Ben	It's nice that you are here in our summer camp, Florian. Are you on holiday here in Bristol?
David	Ben sagt, dass es schön ist, dass du im Sommercamp bist. Bist du hier in Bristol in Urlaub? (2 P)
Florian	Ja, ich bin für zwei Wochen hier. Ich wohne im Haus meiner Tante hier in Bristol.
David	He says that he is here for two weeks. He is staying at his aunt's house here in Bristol. (2 P)
Ben	And where does his/your aunt live?
David	Und wo wohnt deine Tante? (1 P)
Florian	Sie wohnt hinter der Kirche in der Cumberland Street Nummer 7.
David	She lives behind the church in 7, Cumberland Street. (2 P)
Ben	Well, that's great. We only live a mile away. We can come here together in the mornings. We always go by bike.
David	Das ist großartig. Wir wohnen nur eine Meile entfernt. Wir können morgens zusammen hierher kommen. Wir kommen immer mit dem Fahrrad. (3 P)
Florian	Ja, das ist eine gute Idee. Wir können auch heute gleich nach dem Summer Camp zusammen nach Hause gehen.
David	He likes the idea. He says we can go home together today after summer camp. (2 P)
Ben	Yes, we can. But now we must help with the lunch. Let's go.

Lerntipp So kannst du **Getting by in English** üben:
- Unterstreiche in der Lösung Sätze, die dir noch nicht so gut gelungen sind.
- Schreibe die Ausdrücke oder Sätze, die du dir merken möchtest, in dein Lernheft.

2 WORDS Irregular verbs

Infinitive	Simple past form	German translation
ride	rode	reiten
get	got	holen, besorgen
teach	taught	lehren
hear	heard	hören
give	gave	geben
see	saw	sehen
speak	spoke	sprechen
fly	flew	fliegen

> **Lerntipp** Irregular verbs
>
> - Überprüfe, ob du alle unregelmäßigen Verben auf kleine Karteikarten geschrieben hast.
> - Überprüfe, ob du alle Wörter richtig geschrieben hast.
> - Lerne sie erneut.

3 GRAMMAR After the first week at the summer camp

On Monday morning we got up (get up) at 7.30 and went (go) to the camp for the first time. There were (be) 40 boys and girls at the camp. Most of them came (come) from Bristol but some of them weren't (not / be) from our school. In the afternoon we worked (work) on the pirate ship. That was (be) great. On Tuesday we didn't work (not / work) on the ship. On Wednesday and Thursday we read (read) stories about pirates. After that we played (play) on our ship and had (have) a really good time. We didn't read (not / read) comics and we didn't stay (not / stay) in bed all day long.

4 GRAMMAR What Ben and David did and what they didn't do

1 They got up at 7.30.
2 They didn't go by train.
3 They went by bike.
4 They worked on a big ship.
5 They didn't watch TV.
6 They met new friends.
7 They didn't play computer games.
8 They read stories about pirates.

> **Lerntipp** Lies im Englischbuch nochmal die Grammar Files 1, 2 und 3 auf den Seiten 133 und 134. Hier findest du Informationen zum **simple past**.
> Bearbeite dann die Polly-Aufgabe auf S. 134.

Unit 1 — Lösungen A

READING

Bristol Times – Back to school

1 What did they do in the summer camp?

Right: picture 1 and 4

2 Right – wrong?

Right: 1, 6   Wrong: 2, 3, 4, 5

> **Lerntipp** So kannst du **Reading Skills** gut üben:
> - Lies den Text langsam und laut.
> - Unterstreiche die Stellen im Text, die du noch nicht so gut verstanden hast.
> - Lies den Text ein weiteres Mal und löse dann die Aufgaben.

LANGUAGE

1 STUDY SKILLS Describing pictures

1 At the bottom of the picture there is the <u>sea</u>.
2 <u>In the middle</u> there is a café.
3 <u>In the foreground</u> a family is sitting <u>in front of</u> the café.
4 <u>On the left</u> a young man <u>is waving</u>.
5 <u>On the right</u> there are two girls. A young boy with a <u>surfboard</u> is walking <u>between</u> them.
6 <u>In the background</u> there is an old <u>building</u>.
7 <u>At the top</u> I can see a <u>plane</u> in the <u>sky</u>.

> **Lerntipp** Describing pictures
> - Lies im Englischbuch die **Skills File Describing pictures** auf S. 123. Beachte vor allem auch den Tipp.
> - Suche dir aus einer Zeitung oder einer Zeitschrift ein geeignetes Bild, klebe es in dein Lernheft und beschrifte es mit den Ausdrücken zur Bildbeschreibung.
> - Schreibe anschließend eine Bildbeschreibung zu deinem eingeklebten Bild.

Welcome back | Lösungen

> **Lerntipp** So kannst du **Writing Skills** üben:
>
> Schreibe einige Sätze, die du dir merken willst, in dein Lernheft. Wenn du noch unsicher beim Schreiben warst, kannst du die Aufgabe nach ein paar Tagen einfach noch einmal machen.

SPEAKING

02 Talking about the holidays

03 Now you

Mr Hall's questions:	Your answers:
Well, where did you go in your holidays?	We went to Italy.
How did you go there?	We went there by car.
How about the weather, was it nice?	The first week was nice and sunny – one day it was over 30 degrees. The next week was cloudy and it rained on one day.
And did you stay in a hotel?	No, we stayed in our caravan.
Did you go to a museum?	When the weather was bad we went to a museum. Its name was Museum of Spaghetti.
How long were you away?	We were away for two weeks.

> **Lerntipp** So kannst du **Speaking Skills** üben:
>
> - Höre den Musterdialog einige Male an.
> - Bei schwierigen Antworten kannst du die Pausentaste drücken und Jennys Antworten nachsprechen.
> - Lerne einige Lösungssätze auswendig. Wiederhole die Aufgabe in ein paar Tagen. Oder schreibe die Lösungssätze in dein Lernheft und wiederhole die Aufgabe nach einiger Zeit.

2 WORDS Irregular simple past forms

Infinitive	Simple past form	German translation
meet	met	sich treffen
shine	shone	scheinen
swim	swam	schwimmen
put	put	setzen, legen
read	read	lesen
eat	ate	essen
ride	rode	reiten
throw	threw	werfen

Lerntipp So kannst du **die unregelmäßigen Verben** gut üben:

Schreibe dir die unregelmäßigen Verben auf kleine Karteikarten (Format A 8, du kannst sie im Schreibwarengeschäft für wenig Geld bekommen). Eine Karteikarte könnte dann etwa so aussehen:

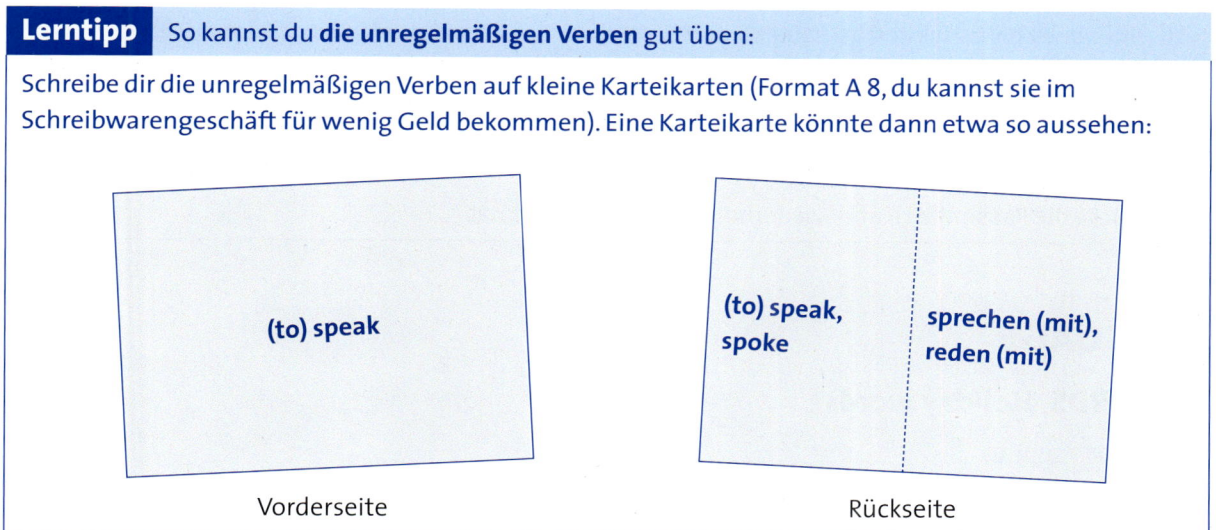

Vorderseite — Rückseite

WRITING

A holiday postcard

1.

Dear Paul,

We are here in Portugal. (1,5 P) We are staying in a nice hotel on the beach. It has got a pool too. (1,5 P) We went swimming in the sea yesterday. The water was super. (1,5 P) Today we want to go on a boat trip. (1,5 P) The weather is great, you know, not too hot. (1,5 P) We are here for one week. (1,5 P)

See you soon. / Lots of love / Love (1 P)

2.

Dear Paul,

London is super!!! (1,5 P) We are staying in a hotel. Mum says it's too loud but I like it. (1,5 P) Yesterday we went to Buckingham Palace and today we want to go shopping in Oxford Street. (3 P) The weather is great, not too cold and not too warm. (1,5 P) We are here for five days. (1,5 P)

See you soon. / Lots of love / Love (1 P)

3 What do you know about Paul's holiday?

		Right	Wrong
1	Paul went on holidays with his parents.	✔	
2	Paul liked the museums in Berlin.		✔
3	Paul can speak French.		✔
4	Paul went to a museum in Munich.	✔	
5	Paul wants to go to Munich again.	✔	
6	The Italians were nice.	✔	
7	Paul didn't like Miami.		✔
8	Paul was in China for one week.		✔
9	Paul's uncle lives in Shanghai.	✔	
10	In Sydney it was wintertime and very cold.		✔

Lerntipp So kannst du **Listening Skills** gut üben:

- Höre dir den Text mehrmals an.
- Drücke die Pausentaste und wiederhole, was Paul gesagt hat.

LANGUAGE

1 WORDS Holiday words

1. Spain is a <u>country</u>.
2. There are three <u>planes</u> in the <u>sky</u>. From up there you have a good <u>view</u>.
3. Is the <u>beach</u> empty? – Yes, there is <u>nobody</u> there.
4. Look, there is a little <u>island</u> in the lake.
5. You live in a country and you go to another country – you go <u>abroad</u>.
6. Every August we stay in our <u>caravan</u> by the <u>sea</u>.
7. Mr and Mrs Miller always <u>fly</u> to Portugal.

Lösungswort: <u>clothes</u>

Lerntipp So kannst du **neue Wörter** gut wiederholen:

- Schau dir im Buch noch einmal die neuen Wörter von "Welcome back" an.
- Schreibe dann bei geschlossenem Buch alle neuen Wörter auf, an die du dich noch erinnerst.
- Vergleiche anschließend mit dem Buch: Hast du alle Wörter richtig geschrieben?
- Wiederhole jetzt besonders die Wörter, die dir nicht mehr eingefallen sind und die du noch nicht richtig geschrieben hast.